© 2013 by Design Media Publishing Limited
This edition published in December 2013

Design Media Publishing Limited
20/F Manulife Tower
169 Electric Rd, North Point
Hong Kong
Tel: 00852-28672587
Fax: 00852-25050411
E-mail: suisusie@gmail.com
www.designmediahk.com

Editing: Tris Green
Proofreading: YIN Qian
Design/Layout: YANG Chunling

P10-p17, P32-p83 Copyright 2006, United Nations Environment Programme
Regional Resource Centre for Asia and the Pacific
P18-p31 Copyright Passive House Institute, http://www.passiv.de/en/

ISBN 978-988-15452-0-6

Printed in China

ECO-HOUSING DESIGN

Edited by Tris Green

Design Media Publishing Limited

004 | **Contents**

ECO-HOUSING PROJECTS

Green, environment-friendly, eco-housing, energy saving, sustainable…the new life style expressed by these words is much of a fad, latest fashion, a trend promoted and advocated by people. In fact, people have been talking about sustainable building methods since the 1970s, it was only in the recent years when internationally recognised ecofriendly house certification systems star ted to function properly.

The first such system was introduced in Great Britain in 1990 - BREEAM or the Building Research Establishment's Environmental Assessment Method. It gained international recognition almost instantly due to the stern assessment criteria and the rather transparent evaluation method.

Although the BREEAM is an internationally recognised system, many European countries developed their own local variations based on the BREEAM standards. In nowadays, EcoHome and LEED are also widely used and gained international recognition. More and more countries' governments, organisations and companies are working on their own fields to promote, study and research eco-housing and energy saving, providing references and standards for eco-and-energy-saving design.

Increase of population and social, economic development result in climate change, which is the biggest threat we face globally. The designer of residential building is responsible for joining in the trend of sustainable design for eco-and-energy-saving houses. Eco-housing involves the followings:

* To fit the new project into the environment by enhancing the natural landscape, not spoiling it.
* Landscaping, to adjust measures to local conditions and choose most suitable solution to maintain existing bio-environment, even enhancing the environment through design.
* To enhance living space quality through available technology, technique, products and design methods to create a comfortable and environment-friendly house with efficient energy saving.

Someone has said that in case a house is energy-saving prior, it must be at the cost of living and aesthetics comfort. I think now he can rest assured that, as more and more manufacturers and suppliers are being devoted to providing a wide range of energy saving products, building materials, decoration materials for architects and interior designers. Here, we select some excellent residential buildings, include house and apartment, which concentrate living and visual comfor t, energy saving and environment protection, completed by architects from several countries for you. On the road back to natural and sustainable development, we will walk forward smoothly.

Introduction of Eco-or-environmental Housing

1. What is Eco-housing?

No precise definition of eco-housing is available. An attempt to define its boundaries at this point of time might risk the premature delivery of an evolving concept. Eco-housing enthusiasts use it to refer to an all-encompassing concept of sustainability of the built environment, achieved through different methods. The most common definitions talk of a comfor table and healthy habitat, achieved by low impact methods, consuming less resource than a standard habitat and using environmental friendly materials and products. Another definition considers eco-housing as a biomimicry by the built environment, imitating the self sustaining and cyclic processes in an ecosystem.

While eco-housing affirms that the basic purpose of buildings is to ensure human comfor t, health and sur vival at an affordable cost, it reminds us that this is best achieved by being in harmony with the ecosystem and the socio-economic system. The use of resources for ensuring human comfort and survival would be done efficiently and effectively, without crossing any thresholds. Similarly the use of nature as a waste sink would be done prudently, without crossing any limits. The usual linear process of extraction-use-disposal would be conver ted to a self sustaining cyclic process.

The definition, criteria and priorities will vary according to site specific factors. Something that is viable in one place may not be viable elsewhere. Several other terms like green buildings, ecological housing, sustainable housing/communities, high performance buildings, environmental architecture etc., are also used in place of ecohousing.

There is also a big overlap between the concepts of eco-housing and Permaculture. Permaculture practitioners study and follow the patterns of nature to develop sustainable patterns of agriculture, land use and habitats, in order to avoid the negative impacts of industrialised agriculture.

World Climate Average:

- Polar
- Temperate
- Arid
- Tropical
- Mediterranean
- Mountains

Box 1: Biomemetics
(Makower, J., 2001, p.20) Biomemetics is a new science that studies the processes in nature, in order to imitate it and design solutions for human problems. An example is studying a leaf to invent a better solar cell. Nature and its constituents have been solving problems for millions of years, out of necessity. Humans could learn a lot by studying it.

2. What are the approaches for achieving eco-housing objectives?

Many specialised tools and techniques could be used for achieving the objectives of ecohousing. Some of the cross-cutting approaches that underlies many of these tools and techniques are: Integrated Design Process; Life Cycle approaches; decreasing resource intensity; bioclimatic design; adopting traditional and local architectural practices; and the use of renewable resources.

2.1 Integrated Design Process

In a conventional design process, each one works within his area of expertise with minimum interaction. The Integrated Design Process is based on inter-disciplinary research and design. Rather than studying the individual building components, systems, or functions in isolation, experts from different disciplines collaborate to analyse the interrelated impacts on the economy, environment, society, building components and materials and find common solutions.

Through their collaborative effort they try to integrate different objectives like economic efficiency, environment friendly site planning, appropriate choices of materials and products, sustainable use of energy and water, provision of clean water, indoor environment quality and sanitation, waste water and solid waste management, and proper operation and maintenance.

Most Desirable

The Waste Management Hierarchy

Prevent Or Reduce Waster Generation

Reuse Waste In Its Current Form

Recycle Waste Into New Products

Treat Waste Before Disposal

Environmentally Safe Disposal

Least Desirable

2.2 Life Cycle Approaches

The traditional compar tmentalised approach considered each stage of a product's life cycle, separately. For example, the manufacturer was not much concerned much with what happened to the product after sales. The environmental manager was unaware of the design and manufacturing issues and used to be preoccupied with "end of pipe" solutions after the waste or pollution was generated. Eco-housing encourages the consideration of the entire life-cycle of the house: from design, through construction, use, maintenance and to end of life activities. Life Cycle thinking takes into account all stages of a buildings existence and considers all stakeholders.

The waste management hierarchy, based on the life cycle thinking, is an important par t of the eco-housing concept. The hierarchy reminds us to act early on in the life cycle of the product to prevent waste generation. The highest priority is for preventing waste generation and the least is for disposal activities. The same concept is applied in the 3R (Reduce, Reuse and Recycle) approach.

Each stage has different characteristics and need different approaches. Eco-housing interventions are more effective during the early phases of the project, as illustrated in figure (facing above) given above.

Figure (Facing above): Influence of design decisions on life-cycle impacts and costs of an average European and Nor th American building (Kohler,N. & Moffatt, S., 2003, p.14).

Life Cycle Assessment or Analysis (LCA) and Life Cycle Costing (LCC) are two of the methodologies used to apply Life Cycle thinking. Among these two, the application of LCA has mostly been limited to research projects due to the large effort and data required. More than the methodologies, the emphasis should be on the contribution of Life Cycle thinking to the Integrated Design Process to take into account all inputs,

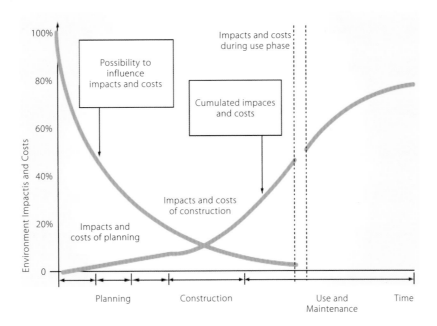

impacts and stakeholders. In few cases Life Cycle thinking may not be appropriate. For example, a project for providing clean water and sanitation for disaster affected people may have the objective of immediate delivery. (Kohler,N. & Moffatt, S., 2003).

2.3 Decreasing Resource Intensity

Experts say that a reduction in resource use by a factor of four is necessary and practical with current levels of technology and knowledge. (Gertsakis. J & Lewis. H, 2003) A bevy of approaches have been promoted in different parts of the world to reduce the flow of primary resources and thereby "dematerialise" the economy. An example is Japan's promotion of the 3R's - Reduce, Reuse, and Recycle.

Eco-housing emphasises the rational use of materials, energy and water. To reduce resource use, the approach discourages use of materials with high resource intensity like concrete and steel. It encourages the use of materials and products with longer lives and needing lesser maintenance. The concept of multifunctional design helps in extending the lifetime of a building, by conver ting or modifying it. Recycling is enabled by deconstruction friendly design and manufacturing. Energy efficiency and load management helps in reducing the energy intensity. Technologies and techniques are available for reducing water use.

But more ambitious proponents of eco-housing propose a move from "dematerialisation" to "rematerialisation". They try to not just reduce resource use and the negative impacts, but imitate natural cycles to create more and more positive impacts such as: "buildings that make oxygen, sequester carbon, fix nitrogen, distill water, provide habitat for thousands of species, accrue solar energy as fuel, build soil, create microclimate, change with the seasons, and are beautiful". They propose a system for continuous tracking of materials and correct recycling and design practices, so that the material can be recycled again and again, unlike current recycling practices, where some material are "downcycled" or recycled few times only. (McDonough, W. & Braungart, M., 2003, p.15)

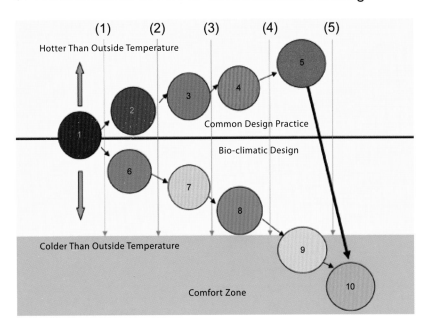

(1). Site elements
(2). Building placement orientation
(3). Envelope component consideration
(4). Indoor environment consideration
(5). Air-conditioning system
1. Climate
2. Micro climate A1
3. Building configuration A2
4. Building envelope A3
5. Designed building A4
6. Micro climate B1
7. Building configuration B2
8. Building envelope B3
9. Passive building B4
10. Desirable building B5

2.4 Bioclimatic Design

2.4.1 What is Bioclimatic Design?

A building provides a passive control over the climate, by separating the interior from the exterior. Additional controls, called active ontrols, can be provided by energy consuming heating, cooling and humidity control systems. One of the aims in ecohousing is to optimise the passive control strategies to achieve comfort conditions and use active controls only if essential. This approach is emphasised in bioclimatic architecture. The main elements in a bioclimatic design are passive.

In contrast, in conventional design the designers do not give much consideration to freely available environmental resources. Instead they rely on active controls to create comfort conditions. The factors affecting human comfort is discussed in the next section.

The following simplified illustration for a warm climate helps to explain bioclimatic design, by contrasting it with the conventional design process. In the bioclimatic design process, the site elements (vegetation and landscape) are used to modify the microclimate. Proper placement and orientation of the building helps to protect itself from sun, wind and rain. It also helps in the optimum use of the sun and wind for ventilation and daylighting. Improvements in the building envelope and emphasis on an improved indoor environment make the interior more comfortable. If the conditions are still short of comfort conditions, a much reduced amount of space conditioning is used.

In the conventional design, most of these factors are neglected making the interior hotter and uncomfor table, compared to the outside. The designer then relies on energy intensive space conditioning to make the interior reach comfort conditions. The figure (Right above) shows the different climatic zone and the comfort zone. As shown in the table (Above), the basic design consideration for the construction of climate responsive buildings in hot and humid climate zones is the use of airflow

Bio-climatic Design Options
(Boonyatikarn, S. & Buranakarn, V., 2006)

Zone	Type	Solution
AA	Very hot	Evaporative cooling
AA	Hot	Evaporative cooling & wind velocity
AA	Hot and humid	Wind velocity
AA	High humidity	Dehumidifying
AA	Very dry	Humidifying
AA	Very cold	Solar radiation

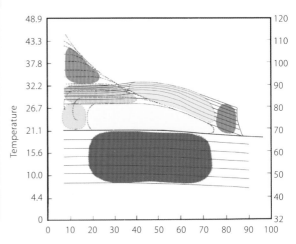

Climate and the comfort zone
(Boonyatikarn, S. & Buranakarn, V., 2006)

to promote heat dissipation by perspiration.

In addition the following are important (UNEP-IETC, 2004):
• Protection from direct solar radiation and preventing undesired heat storage
• Proper rainwater drainage and ventilation to prevent damage from moisture Penetration

Bioclimatic design varies from one climatic zone to the other. A building designed for a hot climate would have measures to reduce the solar gain such as, smaller window sizes; shaded walls; minimum exposure to the west and east; external wall and roof insulation; or use of design elements like solar chimneys, wind towers, etc., to maximise ventilation.

The humidity levels of a climatic zone govern the use of water-based measures for cooling of buildings. While measures like water bodies, fountains, and roof gardens are conducive for a hot-dry climate, these should be used with caution in a humid climatic zone. Even within the same climatic zone, there needs to be distinctions in the design. Each building site would have distinct topography, vegetation, wind-flow pattern, solar and daylight access. The design should be able to address these site conditions and requirements.

2.4.2 What are the factors affecting human comfort? (Szokolay, S V., 2001, p.97-98)
The basic function of a building is to ensure human survival, health and comfort, by protecting it from the external environment. It can be considered as the third skin, the second being our clothes.

Environmental and physiological factors affecting human comfort (Boonyatikarn, S. & B uranakarn, V., 2006) :
1. Air Temperature Humidity
2. Humidity
3. Mean Radiant Temperature
4. Air Velocity
5. Clo Value
6. Metabolism Rate

Humans require thermal, visual and acoustic comfort conditions. Thermal comfort depends on six environmental and physiological factors:
• Air temperature
• Relative Humidity
• Temperature of surrounding surfaces
• Air velocity
• Clothing
• Metabolic rate

These factors are influenced by several other factors:
• Topography: It affects wind movement
• Water bodies: They have high heat storage capacity and this helps to balance the day and night temperature variation.
• Altitude: Air temperature decreases with increasing altitude, by approximately 2°C for every 300m.
• Vegetation: Affects all aspects of the micro climate .
• Level of urbanisation: The more the built surfaces, the more the heat island effect.
• Ground surface: Different surfaces have different heat storing and reflecting capacity and water content and hence affect the surrounding temperature differently. Light coloured surfaces reflect most of the heat. Rocks absorb heat during day time and release it during the night.
Vegetations absorb heat, but remain cool, due to the evaporation from the leaves.
• Age and Sex: Metabolic activity of older people, women and children are generally lesser.
• Level of Activi... It affects the metabolic rate.

Box 2: The boa,   *mechanism*
(Szokolay, S V., 2
For survival, humc   *should be around 35~40°C, and the skin*

temperature should be 31~34°C. When outside temperature is too low, heat loss takes place from our body. If outside temperature is too high, then our body gains heat from outside. The bodies internal thermo-regulation mechanism, maintains the body temperature for all normal variations in climate. Further protection is provided by the clothing and building envelope.

If the body has to retain heat (if the outside is too cold), the blood vessels contract (vascular contraction) and less blood flows towards the skin and less heat loss takes place from the body to the outside. In extreme cold conditions, we also shiver, which is a heat generating mechanism, supplementing the normal thermo-regulation mechanism. If the body needs to loose heat (if outside is too warm), then the blood vessels dilate (vascular dilation) and more blood flows towards the skin and more heat loss takes place to the outside. Sweating is a supplementary mechanism to loose heat.

2.5 Adopting Traditional And Local Architectural Practices

Many ancient architectural traditions promoted habitats that were sustainable. Examples are the Chinese "Feng Shui" and the Indian "Vastu Vidya". They were based on a proper understanding of bioclimatic conditions, and sustainable patterns of living. Educated people look at these traditions with suspicion, due to their association with religion. We could gain much by rediscovering and demystifying these traditions. (CIB & UNEPIETC, 2002) Traditional wisdom is partly reflected in the practices in use in many local communities. Traditional building methods cannot be simply copied, but needs to be adapted to make it relevant to modern realities. They could also form the basis for developing more sustainable technologies.

2.6 Using Renewable Resources

The use of renewable materials and energy helps in reducing the use of non-renewable resources. This is sustainable as long as the rate of extraction of the renewable resource does not exceed its rate of regeneration and does not cause adverse effects, such asenvironmental impacts or shortages in food production.

3. Passive House

3.1 What is a Passive House?

Passive House is a building standard that is truly energy efficient, comfortable and affordable at the same time. Passive House is not a brand name, but a tried and true construction concept that can be applied by anyone, anywhere.

Yet, a Passive House is more than just a low-energy building:

- Passive Houses allow for energy savings of up to 90% compared with typical Central European building stock and over 75% compared to average new builds. Passive Houses use less than 1.5 l of oil or 1.5m³ of gas to heat one square meter of living space for a year – substantially less than common "low-energy" buildings. Vast energy savings have been demonstrated in warm climates where typical buildings also require active cooling.
- Passive Houses make efficient use of the sun, inter nal heat sources and heat recover y, rendering conventional heating systems unnecessary throughout even the coldest of winters. During warmer months, Passive Houses make use of passive cooling techniques such as strategic shading to keep comfortably cool.
- Passive Houses are praised for the high level of comfort they offer. Internal surface temperatures vary little from indoor air temperatures, even in the face of extreme outdoor temperatures. Special windows and a building envelope consisting of a highly insulated roof and floor slab as well as highly insulated exterior walls keep the desired warmth in the house – or undesirable heat out.
- A ventilation system imperceptibly supplies constant fresh air, making for superior air quality without unpleasant draughts. A highly efficient heat recovery unit allows for the heat contained in the exhaust air to be re-used.

Passive House – building for energy efficiency, comfort and affordability.
Typical heating systems in Central Europe, where the Passive House Standard was first developed and applied, are centralised hot water heating systems consisting of radiators, pipes and central oil or gas boilers. The average heating load of standard

buildings in this area is approximately $100W/m^2$ (approx. 10kW for a 100m² apartment). The Passive House concept is based on the goal of reducing heat losses to an absolute minimum, thus rendering large heating systems unnecessary. With peak heating loads below 10W per square metre of living area, the low remaining heat demand can be delivered via the supply air by a post heating coil. A building that does not require any heating system other than post air heating is called a Passive House, since no active heating (or cooling) system is needed.

3.2 Passive Houses around the World
The Passive House concept itself remains the same for all of the world's climates, as does the physics behind it. Yet while Passive House principles remain the same across the world, the details do have to be adapted to the specific climate at hand. A building fulfilling the Passive House Standard will look much different in Alaska than in Zimbabwe.

Passive Houses: a method rather than a building style
In Central European Climate there is a lot of practical experience on how to build Passive Houses. But it would be a pitfall just to apply the Central European Passive House design, especially the details used for insulation, windows and ventilation and just copy these to a completely different situation because there is a specific building tradition in every country and there are specific climatic boundary conditions in every region. Therefore, the specific solution for a Passive House has to be adapted to the country and the climate under consideration. On the other hand, the goals are the same in all climates and for all countries. Also, physics is the same all around the world. So the problem to build almost self sufficient houses (i.e. Passive Houses) is well defined. The physical equations are the same - only the boundary conditions vary. Thus the solution method can well be applied independently of the circumstances in order to find the appropriate way of Passive House design in a specific country and climate.

3.3 Passive Houses: The Functional Definition

It is a lucky coincidence: Although the specific design of passive houses may look quite different in varying circumstances, the leading principle will be the same. This principle has been derived from Amory Lovins' idea of reducing the investment by using a more energy efficient design, going that far with efficiency, that there will be a certain breakthrough to radically simplified technology.

For the case of heating or cooling, this means to radically reduce the peak load by means of insulation, heat recovery, highly insulating windows, passive solar design and other measures. When the peak heating load reaches the value of $10W/m^2$, independently of the climate, the ventilation system may easily be used for heating. No other heat distribution system than just the air supplied for excellent indoor air quality is required any more. Thus, the definition of a Passive House basically consists of limiting the peak heating load to $10W/m^2$. In some climates that may be easy to achieve; in other, colder climates it may be more difficult. And the same applies for cooling: Passive measures are to be chosen to reduce the peak cooling load: proper size and quality of windows and shading und the reduction of the internal heat loads by using highly energy efficient equipment. Again, the remaining small amount of cooling energy which might still be needed can be delivered by cooling of the fresh air supply required for good indoor air quality anyhow (See Passive Houses in South-West Europe as a exemplary solution).

3.4 Practical Hints

Looking at the heating load is just an example. In many locations other energy services such as cooling or dehumidification are more important. Again the method to determine a Passive House will be the same: Peak loads are limited until an appreciable simplification of the active technology needed for cooling/ dehumidification can be achieved.

Some rules of thumb which are valid for all climates:

- You should keep comfort at a high level. Passive Houses should be well known as the most comfor table houses – in any country and within any climate. Be aware that all persons would like to live in a comfortable indoor climate and that all of them should have a right to do so. Therefore, in the long run, no solution will persist which will not contribute to a better indoor climate.

- The solution should be simpler than ordinary buildings/systems used so far. Only affordable solutions will be attractive in a competition with conventional technology like standard air conditioning.

- It is not necessary that the solution will not need any conventional energy demand ("zero energy solution") – that might be very expensive. It is sufficient to use a lot less energy than in ordinary systems. At a factor of 4 to 10, the energy conservation is likely to be high enough
to pay for the extra efforts needed.

- Insulation might be a good idea in all climates.

- Shading will be absolutely necessary in all climates with high solar radiation during Summer.

- Heat recovery will be necessar y in all cold and in all hot climates. If the houses have a ventilation system, which will be a good idea if external temperature will be lower than 8°C or higher than 32°C in a relevant time period, the supply air ducts may well be used to transport heat during the heating season, cool air during the hot periods and dry air to dehumidify if necessary.

- Using very low amounts of auxiliary energy is an important precondition for passive solutions. The fans in ventilation systems, for example, must use highly efficient electronically commutated motors. This is obvious in the case of recovery of cooling energy, but it is necessary in systems for heat recovery, too. On the other hand – don't hesitate to use a ventilator ; moving air requires much less energy than heating or cooling it significantly.

- In many cases the ground can be used as a heat or cold buffer. Vernacular architecture in a country may indicate whether ground coupled systems are an oppor tunity. The traditional solution may be very expensive, however – like huge air channels or earth buried houses; that will not be a solution reproducible for the future. But there are less expensive solutions using modern technology like earth buried ducts or ground probes.

3.5 Technical and Economic Aspects

Preliminary requirements for residential Passive Houses in all climates worldwide were derived from the technical and economic considerations. These requirements concern indoor heating, sensible and latent cooling, airtightness and primary energy demand. The criteria for primary energy demand and airtightness remained the same worldwide.

3.5.1 Passive House in Warm Climates

Various questions have to be posed when looking at Passive Houses in warm climates. How can Passive Houses be built in warm climates such as the Mediterranean climate and what strategies are reasonable? What is the respective impact of different design parameters? What performance level of components is required for the building envelope and mechanical services? And what challenges does this pose on the component industry? First realized projects and various studies can already give some answers.

The Passive Houses discussed in this article are located in warm, but not hot, and mainly dry regions, with annual mean temperatures between 15°C and 23°C and no dehumidification demand all year round. The highest monthly mean dew point temperature is 16°C (Volos, Greece). This comprises climates that are warmer than the central European climate, such as most regions in Spain and Italy. Included, but a somewhat special case are so-called "happy" or "easy" climates. These are zones where the situation all year round is so mild and advantageous that comfortable

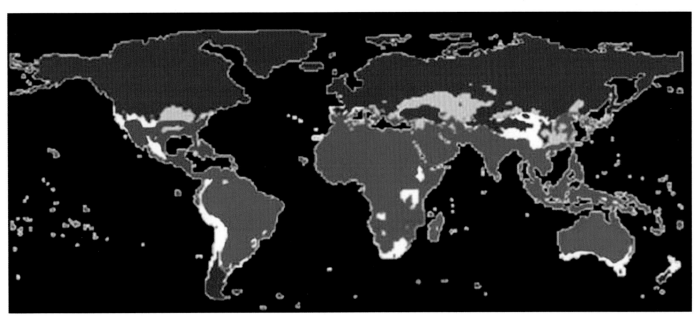

indoor conditions can be easily achieved, without or with very little energy demand. Examples are the area around the city Guadalajara, Mexico, as well as most par ts of Portugal, see the figure (Above).

Figure: White Regions with warm, moderate climate (depending on altitude), where it is relatively easy to achieve Passive House ("Happy climates").

Source: Passive House Institute

Warm and humid climates, like the climate of Seoul, South Korea, which is warm but also has two humid months, as well as more extreme climates such as the hot climates of Las Vegas, US, Shanghai, China, and Tokyo, Japan, are not covered in this ar ticle. They are analysed in the studies [Schulz 2012] and [Feist 2012]. Certified Passive House examples in those regions can be found in the Passive House Database.

Conclusion

First certified Passive Houses in warm climates show the optimisation potential in design and execution. While lower levels of insulation are sufficient for moderate and warm climates such as the majority of the Mediterranean region, high levels of insulation in opaque elements of the building envelope are required for extremely hot climates. To achieve cost-efficient solutions, the resulting insulation thicknesses call for optimised compactness of the building shape. Windows should meet the comfort and energy requirements, and the designer should be aware of the high influence of the best orientation. Very good air tightness is important in all climates, and especially for hot and humid climates [Schnieders et. al. 2012]. Active cooling could be avoided in so-called "Happy climates", but is mandatory for very warm climates (for instance Granada, Spain). Ventilation strategies include natural ventilation in summer as well as mechanical ventilation (extract air system only or ventilation system with heat exchanger and summer bypass). For cost effective Passive Houses in warm climates component performance should be in the focus of all stakeholders.

3.5.2 Passive House in Mixed Humid Climates

Comprehensive studies carried out by the Passive House Institute have lead to the following findings/recommendation for the construction of Passive House buildings in mixed humid climates, i.e. in such climates which will require heating, cooling and dehumidification. Boundary conditions for mixed humid climates: The climate is dominated by cooling, with some 5 to 10 kKh of cooling degree hours and high humidity for some months, so that a significant amount of energy is required for dehumidification. Nonetheless, heating also plays a role at around 50kKh heating degree hours. The "classic" Passive House approach performs quite well here and basically offers two benefits: it reduces the heating load in winter and the cooling load in summer.

Insulation is the most important factor. U-values of around $0.15W/(m^2K)$ (roof) and $0.20W/(m^2K)$ (outer wall) reduce demand for heat considerably and improve the cooling load and demand for cooling energy. Further improvements are hardly necessary (lower costs). Insulation to the ground is not crucial and sometimes even irrelevant, as is the case for the thermal separation of foundations. If they are "within" the ground area as much as possible, there is no need to avoid strips and piles in the foundations. Instead, an "insulation apron" (some 50-100cm around the perimeter) can help.

Excellent air tightness is very important here to prevent damage:
• Moist air exiting from inside in the winter (as in central Europe) can cause condensation damage in the wall.
• Very humid air entering from outside in the summer (additional burden on indoor air climate) can also cause condensation damage in the wall as the interior is cooled.

Triple or double low-e glazing may be advantageous, as the case may be. Triple low-e glazing usually increases savings for heating energy in the winter. In cooling, the main benefit comes from sun protection thanks to the lower g-value.

Windows should face the south and north. This classic Passive House wisdom is even more important at the 31st parallel than north of the Alps. So buildings should be oriented so that the main façades face south/north – if possible. Larger West and East facing windows will need a temporary shading device to prevent the rooms from overheating. Large windows tend to increase the cooling load, so don't make them too big. Windows that make up 30% of the façade are by far enough. Please note that a square meter of window area is significantly more expensive than a square metre of opaque wall.

Overhangs are a good way of shading southern/northern windows. Overhangs also, however, increase heating demand (if there is any). The optimal compromise is overhangs reaching out 1 to 1.5m. The simulation clearly shows that solar protective glazing considerably reduces cooling demand, with heating demand increasing slightly. This latter shortcoming may be compensated easily in compact buildings (low surface/ volume ratio), without having to resort to thick layers of insulation. Of course, variable outdoor shading (blinds) would be even better than solar protective glazing. But note: movable blinds are relatively expensive and are sometimes not applicable because of risk of high wind velocity in some regions. In addition blinds must be operated "correctly", i.e. they need to be closed to block intense solar radiation present in hot periods. As users may not be expected to operate the blinds correctly all the time, shadings might be open too long during hot periods. Interior shading is not recommended because it only reduces solar loads by around 35% and therefore an excessive fraction of solar radiation enters the building and increases the demand for cooling energy considerably.

Insulated window frames are not needed in these climates; a narrow conventional frame suffices. The frame must, however, be air tight and have no thermal bridges to prevent moisture from damaging the building.

Mechanical ventilation is a MUST almost everywhere. Many building owners are already aware of this requirement; in the hot periods, outdoor air is often so humid that direct window ventilation can cause unpleasant humidity, create condensation on surfaces, and increase the need for dehumidification. Users therefore rarely open windows. To provide good indoor air quality under these circumstances, a mechanical ventilation system is needed.

Our findings show that heat recovery (at least around 75 percent efficiency) clearly reduces demand for heating energy, though power is needed for ventilators. The resulting primary energy savings are only significant if the systems consume very little power! Of course this is only relevant in climates with a noteworthy heating demand.

In smaller residential units ($<50m^2$), heat recovery is better from a central system (such as on the roof of each staircase). This approach is much less expensive and facilitates maintenance. During hot periods, fresh air is first cooled and dehumified centrally (to around 20°C, with the dew point being below 16°C) before it is conditioned again as needed individually for each apartment with an auxiliary cooling register for circulating air. This semicentral concept for ventilation cooling and dehumification is the most promising (facing). The central unit compensates for pressure losses at the central system and in distribution pipes, making the system highly efficient. Individual apartments "request" the fresh air and send the extract air out through the central duct driven by small, highly efficient ventilators. Only a heating/cooling register or a (small) classic circulation cooling unit needs to be installed in each apartment. But don't forget the condensate drain!

In hot periods ventilation/heat recovery has to be adjusted according to the outdoor climate. Sometimes, outdoor air can be used directly for cooling and dehumidification without heat and moisture recovery. A controlled, adjustable bypass is therefore highly recommended. It is advisable to optimise both the hardware design and the control strategy for air conditioning in a dynamic simulation.

The heat recovery devices have to include moisture recovery with an efficiency of at

Diagram of individual zones in the simula tion model (Dynbil)

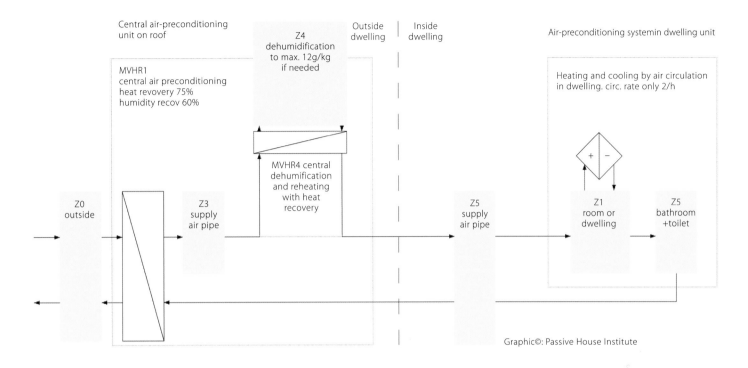

Graphic©: Passive House Institute

least 60 % in humid climates. In the summer, this approach considerably reduces the dehumidification load in such climates, since moisture recover y helps to keep the high outdoor humidity outside the building. A large fraction of outside air humidity thus passes from the outside back to the outside. Energy only needs to be used for the downstream dehumidification of fresh air to remove the remaining excess moisture. The strategy is to dehumidify the air a bit more than necessary to create an additional "buffer" for moisture sources inside.

Excursus: Solely fresh air cooling concept – no circulation air in apartment.

Please note: Fresh air cooling is theoretically possible but fur ther investigations are needed to check air inlet temperatures and related effects of discomfort.

If the maximum cooling load can be reduced to around 8 W/m², cooling via precooled fresh air would be possible with a supply air exchange rate of around 0.4 1/h. Cooling coils have to be installed in each apartment. Central precooling is set to around 16 °C. Air is heated up to around 23 °C in the central network before it reaches the apartment. There, the air can be cooled down again with cold water (at around 2 °C – warning: insulate water lines and air tubes to avoid condensation). In addition, some recirculated room air, about the same airflow volume as the supply air, may pass across the cooling coil. This provides some leeway for excess cooling loads. This cooling concept based solely on fresh air entails a risk in that fresh air temperatures are much lower than with conventional circulating air coolers. Specifically, fresh air outlets can reduce comfort during cooling. There exist some general ideas about how to design air inlets for this cooling regime, but additional experimental research must be done to see how far fresh air temperature can be reduced at the fresh air valve without reducing comfort.

For the proposed cooling concept with circulation cooling a time resolved dynamic thermal simulation was carried out for a special building located in Southern China with small apar tments and hotel rooms. The results show that the maximum cooling load in an apar tment is 11W/m² and the dehumidification load is 6W/m² with an occupancy of only one person per apartment/hotel room (20m²). With centrally preconditioned air (cooled and dehumidified, 16°C and passively reheated to 22°C) coming to the apartments, just one small, conventional circulation cooler per apartment is the easiest way to meet the remaining cooling and dehumidification load.

If the circulation share in addition to supply air ventilation rate of 0.4 1/h is increased to around 2 1/h (which is low compared to conventional circulation cooling units), the cooling load can be handled even at fresh (preconditioned) air temperatures of around 20-23°C. Fur thermore, acceptance of the technology will probably not be a problem, since circulation coolers are a conventional technology well known in the hotel sector. The elegant thing about this concept is that the (circulation) heat exchanger can be used for both cooling and heating. At a heating load of around 7W/m², water temperatures of 42°C are sufficient. Ground probes can provide or support recooling in hot periods and serve as a heat source in cold periods, thereby acting as both a heat source or heat sink as needed. Ground probes need to be dimensioned sufficiently large, which is easier at smaller energy demand. For Passive buildings, far fewer boreholes are needed because the heating and cooling loads in Passive Houses are much lower. The system is therefore less expensive.

Please Note: Direct cooling from ground heat exchangers, with flow temperatures of the cooling fluid similar to the ground temperature has proven to work well in cool climates, but is not feasible in climates with annual average temperatures above 15°C. In such climates a central cooling unit with an additional heat pump must be installed. This system provides each apar tment with cold water (around 2°C) in the hot periods and hot water (around 45°C) in cold periods. For more notes: The same network can be used for heating and cooling because in Passive Houses the heating and cooling seasons do not overlap – there is always an intermediate period in between because of the long time constant of such well insulated buildings.

Wall composition and materials selected:
There may be large vapor pressure and temperature differences between outside and inside because of high relative humidity of outdoor air during hot and humid periods, with indoor air being cooled and dehumidified at the same time. Then, moisture buildup in the structure of the wall may occur. This is of particular concern if mineral wool is used, which has a low resistance to vapour diffusion.

For mineral wool ETICS systems, take care that the outside rendering is made from non pouros cement so that the rendering layer doesn't accumulate much water during nighttime or rainfall. This is because some of the water absorbed in the outer render will be driven towards the cooled (25°C) inside surface as soon as solar radiation begins to heat up the render. In addition, the render must be open for vapour diffusion to allow drying of the insulation layer behind. EPS, as an alternative material with less humidity problems, is not allowed because of fire protection requirements.

Another possible solution is the use of porous concrete. Its hygroscopic proper ties allow to absorb and buffer large amounts of condensation and support drying of the matrix. Hygrothermal simulations have shown that such a wall structure works well in a mixed humid climate. Unfortunately, porous concrete is hard to handle on the building site because it is very fragile.

Please note: These questions cannot be seen as completely solved yet in all climatic bounary conditions, please be careful when designing external building elements for this type of climate. This needs careful further investigations and namely more experimental evidence.

3.6 Passive House Requirements

A building is a Passive House if it meets the following three criteria:

3.6.1 A comfor table indoor climate is achievable without a separate heating system and without an air conditioning system: for this the annual heating demand may not exceed 15 kWh/(m²a) in accordance with the Passive House Planning Package (PHPP).

3.6.2 The criteria for thermal comfort must be met for all living areas during winter as well as in summer.

The following requirements arise from this:
- U-values of opaque exterior components must be less than 0.15 W/(m²K).
- U-values of windows and other translucent building components must be less than 0.8 W/(m²K).
- Translucent areas oriented towards the west or east (±50°) and translucent areas inclined at an angle of 75° to the horizontal may not exceed 15% of the useful areas behind these or they must be equipped with temporary solar protection with a reduction factor of at least 75%. For south-oriented windows the limit is 25% of the useful areas behind these.
- The supply air temperatures at the air outlet in the room must not be below 17°C. Consistently uniform flow of air through all areas and into all rooms must be ensured (ventilation efficiency). The ventilation must be dimensioned primarily for air hygiene (DIN 1946). Noise emission from the ventilation system must be minimal (<25 dBA).
- Houses must have at least one openable opening for outdoor air in each room; air flow through the home must be possible (free cooling in summer).

**Basic Principles for the Construction
of Passive Houses:**
1. Thermal insulation
2. Passive house windows
3. Comfort ventilation with
   highly heat recovery
4. Airtightness
5. Thermal-bridge-free

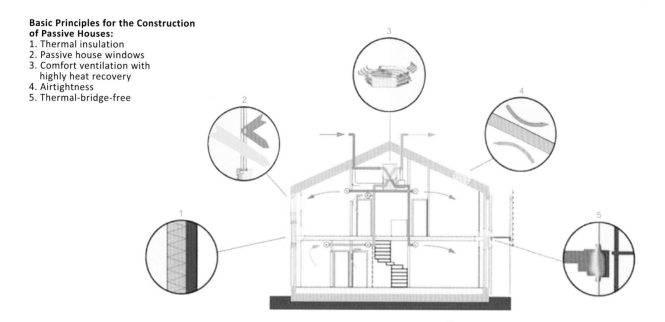

3.6.3 The use of specific primary energy for all domestic applications (heating, hot water and domestic electricity) must not exceed 120 kWh/(m²a) in total. The calculation is carried out in accordance with the PHPP.

The following basic principles apply for the construction of Passive Houses:

Thermal Insulation

All opaque building components of the exterior envelope of the house are so well-insulated that they have a heat transfer coefficient (U-value) of 0.15W/(m-K) at the most, i.e. a maximum of 0.15 watts per degree of temperature difference and per square metre of exterior surface are lost.

Passive House Windows

The windows (glazing together with the window frame) should not exceed a U-value of 0.80 W/(m-K), with g-values around 50% (g-value=total solar transmittance, proportion of the solar energy available for the room).

Ventilation Heat Recovery

Convenience ventilation with highly effective heat recovery firstly allows for a good quality of indoor air, and secondly it helps to save energy. In the Passive House at least 75% of the heat from the exhaust air is transferred to the fresh air again by means of a heat exchanger.

Air Tightness of the Building

Uncontrolled leakage through gaps must be smaller than 0.6 of the total house volume per hour during a test with a negative pressure/excess pressure of 50 Pascal.

Absence of Thermal Bridges

All edges, corners, connections and penetrations must be planned and executed with great care, so that thermal bridges can be avoided. Thermal bridges which cannot be avoided must be minimised as far as possible.

Guidelines for Eco-housing

1. Pre-design Guidelines
• Select an effective, multi-disciplinary design team. The team could include the owner, architects, engineers and subject-specific experts.
• Make an assessment of the existing socio-cultural, environmental and economic condition of the locality. The project needs to use and maximise the existing potential.
• Develop a vision statement. The vision statement should clearly set out the goals, objectives, and processes. It should be based on the site assessment, resource availability, available best practices and technologies, and cost-effectiveness. The project must also identify if the design goals intend to achieve improvements over the conventional standards, e.g., better envelope standards than minimum energy codes, better water efficiency than the national codes.

The goals needs to be prioritized based on the needs and project constraints, e.g., water quality and conservation may be a priority in tsunami-affected regions.
• Develop an action plan, budget and time schedule .
• Finalise appropriate procedures for contracting and contractor selection. Appropriate guidelines, specifications and procedures should be laid within the contract document to meet eco-design objectives.
• Try to ensure that all stakeholders are involved in different aspects of the project planning and implementation, to ensure that all factors are considered and to increase the acceptability of the project.
• Develop simple indicators for regular monitoring and evaluation of the project progress and for social and environmental impacts of the project.
• Develop a strategy to mitigate risks due to any possible disruptions to the achievement of the project goals.

2. Site Planning
Sustainable site planning involves proper site selection, site assessment and site development.

2.1 Site Selection

• Avoid using sites having special value like agricultural land, cultural sites, wetlands, habitats of endangered species etc.

• Reuse land that has already been developed or a more ambitious target could be to reuse land that is polluted.

• Give special considerations for disaster prone areas. For example in a tsunami prone area, the site should be out of the safety buffer zone, at an elevated place, preferably not on slopes or near other steep slopes and should avoid different floor levels.

2.2 Site Assessment

An assessment should be made of the site's potential to provide natural resources such as solar energy, light, water etc and the possible impacts of the project on these features. It would result in the modification of the site layout and the building design, to maximize the use of these natural resources and to protect them from deterioration. It would ensure minimum site disruption; maximum usage of bio-climatic features; minimum requirement for intra/inter-site transportation; appropriate erosion and sedimentation control plans; and appropriate landscaping. The guidelines for achieving these are as follows:

• Collect data of the geographic coordinates, topography and bioclimatic features of the site. Test air, soil and ground water quality, to ensure that no deterioration occurs to the quality as a result of the project.

• Check water quality to assess the need for accessing other cleaner sources or for establishing water treatment facilities.

• Check the depth of the ground water table. This would help to decide the depth and size of the foundation, and the depth and distance between the septic and water tanks.

• Assess soil quality, which is an important information for deciding the shape of foundation, constructing septic tanks and for accessing ground water.

• Study the existing pattern of native vegetation. Ensure that the design and construction does not result in any damage to the vegetation or their ability to survive.

• Identify the tr aditional style of a rchitecture and the existing form of the city or village. The new construction should as much as possible, blend with the existing situation and use their positive features.

• Study the history of natural disasters in the locality and the design could factor in such possibilities.

• Identify the damage rever sals that need to be addressed prior to implementation of the eco-housing project, e.g., measures for tackling salt contamination and groundwater contamination in tsunami affected areas. List out the actions that are required to address these issues.

• Assess the accessibility to infrastructure and conveniences such as power supply, water supply, sanitation, waste management, roads, shops, schools, hospitals, markets and employment opportunities.

• Make an assessment of the costs of construction at the locality, including the land price, cost of land filling, costs for providing basic infrastructure, cost of building material etc.

• Decide on which kind of infrastructure system to apply at the site: centralised or decentralised.

• Prepare a list of laws, codes, standards, best practices and incentives/ penalties. These could include:

- Building codes, laws and regulations such as minimum distance between houses, minimum size of plots, minimum plot density, purpose and use of building, street width, height of building and number of storeys etc.

- Codes, laws and regulations related to water and waste management and use of renewable energy, etc.

- Environmental clearances required, if any.

- Disaster mitigation measures.

- Energy codes/standards.

- Relevant building codes.

- Applicable international and national best practices as identified in project goal.
- Financial incentives for eco-measures, e.g., subsidies for renewable energy systems and energy-efficient equipment.

2.3 Site Development
2.3.1 Site Layout
• Ensure that basic amenities such as bank, child care, post office, park, library, convenience grocery, primary school, clinic and community hall are near to or within the site premises.
• Make a comprehensive transpor tation plan for the site, taking into consideration cleaner transpor tation options, parking capacity and conveniences for pedestrians and cyclists. All external traffic and pollution should end at the entrance of the site or the parking space.
Discourage use of fossil fuel-based vehicles, on site. Plan pedestrian access ways and bicycle tracks within site premises.
• Analyse the existing roads and pathways on site, to reduce the length of roads and utility lines.
• The site layout should allow for wind protection and solar access in winter and adequate sun protection and ventilation in summer. Having a mix of building types could help achieve this.
• Row buildingscanbeusedaswindbreakers. High-rise can increase ventilation in a dense development. Low-rise buildings should be sited so that they avoid excessive heat exchange with the environment and utilise their link with open spaces. Wherever possible, open spaces and the funnel effect should be used to increase airflow within buildings.
• The ratio of street width to building height determines the altitude up to which solar radiation can be cut off. Similarly, street orientation determines the azimuth up to which solar radiation can be cut off. These two factors should be optimized on large sites. But for warm humid climates, the main aim is to have air movement. Hence the streets should be oriented to utilise the natural wind patterns.

• Site should be properly planned to mitigate the 'heat island effect by reducing the total paved area allowed. The paved areas should be made pervious or open grid. Shading should be provided or the paved surfaces.

• Use gravity systems for water supply and sewer age , wherever possible, to avoid pumping.

• Try to locate all utility lines near already disturbed areas, like roads. Use concealed or shielded conduits for utility lines.

• Optimise the layout, to save land and natural resources, without affecting the quality of life.

• The layout should be flexible to accommodate future changes that could arise from the users needs or from other perspectives.

• The layout should use innovative ways to facilitate social networks among the residents. These could include the provision of parks, recreational areas, community halls etc.

2.3.2 Landscaping

• For projects larger than one hectare, remove topsoil and preserve for reuse on site. For tsunami affected areas, ensure that the topsoil has not been rendered unusable. A pH of 6.0 to 7.5 and organic content of not less than 1.5% by mass, needs to be maintained. Add lime where pH is less than 6.0. Use organic compost and mychorrizal biofertiliser for remediation of alkaline soil, as is the case with soil affected by sea water intrusion. Any soil having soluble salt content greater than 500ppm should not be used for the purpose of landscaping.

• The most effective way to prevent soil erosion, sedimentation, and to stabilise soil is through the provision of vegetative cover by effective planting practices The foliage and roots of plants provides dust control and a reduction in soil erosion by increasing infiltration, trapping sediments, stabilising soil, and dissipating the energy of hard rain. Temporar y seeding can be used in areas disturbed after rough grading to provide soil protection until the final cover is established.

Permanent seeding/planting is used in buffer areas, vegetated swales, and steep

Case (a)

Case (b)

Case (a):
Tall trees might result in loss of wind as it gets deflected.
Case (b):
Small dense trees would guide the wind towards houses.

slopes. The vegetative cover also increases the percolation of rainwater thereby increasing the groundwater recharge.

• Selection of plant species should be based on its water requirements and the micro climatic benefits that would result from it. Deciduous trees provide shade in summer and allow sunlight in winter. Evergreen trees provide shade and wind control throughout the year.

• Preserve existing vegetation on site. Mark all the existing vegetation in a tree survey plan. Evolve tree preservation guidelines. Replant within the site premises any mature trees that have been removed, in the ratio of 1:5. At the same time, care needs to be taken to avoid undesirable increase in humidity levels, by excessive plantations.

• Composting and plant wastes should be preferred to chemical fertilisers. They would also reduce the need for pesticides.

• Do not alter the existing drainage pattern on site. Existing grades should be maintained around existing vegetation. Ensure that the vegetation remains healthy.

• Use of organic mulches has to be done to enhance soil stabilisation. Organic mulches include shredded bark, wood chips, straw, composted leaves, etc. Inorganic mulches such as pea gravel, crushed granite, or pebbles can be used in unplanted areas. Stone mulches should not be used adjacent to the building as they can easily get heated and cause glare. Mulching is good for stabilising soil temperature also. The coarser the material, the deeper should it be applied.

• Sedimentation basins, and contour trenching, also helps top reduce soil erosion.

• Some methods for altering the air flow patterns by landscaping are shown in the figures above.

3. Building Materials and Products

Eco-friendly materials are characterised by low-embodied energies, low emissions and are convenient for recycling and reuse. Building materials are mostly made from naturally available materials like clay, stone, sand or biomass. Proper selection of building materials would help to conserve these natural resources.

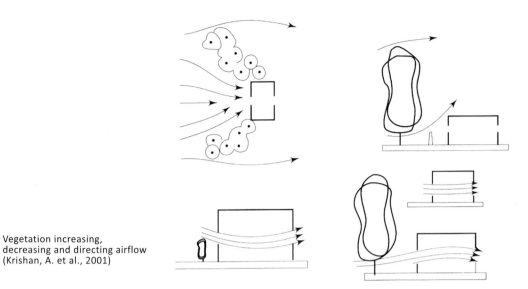

Vegetation increasing,
decreasing and directing airflow
(Krishan, A. et al., 2001)

Wastes and byproducts generated from various manufacturing processes could form secondary resources for production of building materials. This would allow savings in consumption of primary grade raw materials, energy, labour, and capital investments in plants. Using local materials could minimise emissions from transport, strengthen the local industries, increases employment for locals, helps avoid taxes on imported material and help in preserving the culture. The selection of appropriate materials is driven by local/regional considerations. A material that is suitable for one place may not be suitable elsewhere. We also need to understand that the building styles and design are heavily influenced by prevailing fashions, especially the fashions in the developed world. This was one of the reasons why many modern construction materials could ease out more durable, climate responsive traditional building materials in the developing world. (UNEP-IETC, 2004, p.27-29) The points to be noted for material and product selection are:

• Use naturally available materials, especially or ganic renewable materials like timber, trees, straw, grass, bamboo etc. Even nonrenewable inorganic materials like stone and clay are useful, since they can be reused or recycled. (UNEP-IETC, 2004, p.27-29)

• Use certified timber. Check the reliability of the certificates, as forgery is possible.

• Do not use sand quar ried from cor al reefs.

• Check or igin of soil for land filling.

• Check whether quarry sites are rehabilitated.

• Use materials with low-embodied energy content for all structural work in fill systems.

• Use locally available materials and technologies, employing local work force.

• Use materials amenable for reuse and recycling. Pure material like bricks, wood, concrete, stone, metal sheets are most suitable for this purpose. Composite materials like prefabricated solid foam-metal or foam-plaster elements are difficult to separate and to recycle.

• Use industrial waste-based bricks/blocks for non-structural or infill wall system.

- Reuse/recycle constr uction debris.
- Minimise use of wood for inter ior wor ks and use any of the following in place of wood.
- Composite wood products such as hardboards, block boards, lumbercore plywood, veneered panels, par ticle boards, medium/low-density fibreboards made from recycled wood scrap from sawmill dusts or furniture industry and bonded with glue or resin under heat and pressure.
- Materials/ products made from rapidly renewable small-diameter trees and fastgrowing, low-utilised species harvested within a ten-year cycle or shor ter, such as bamboo, rubber, eucrasia, eucalyptus, poplar, jute/cotton stalks, etc. The products include engineered products, bamboo ply boards, rubber, jute stalk boards, etc.
- Products made from wastes. These could be wood waste, agricultural wastes, and natural fibres, such as sisal, coir, and glass fibre in inorganic combination with gypsum, cement, and other binders, such as fibrous gypsum plaster boards, etc.
- Salvaged timber and reused wood products such as antique furniture.
- Use water-based acrylics for paints.
- Use acrylics, silicones, and siliconized acrylic sealants for interior use.
- Use adhesives with no/low Volatile Organic Compound (VOC) emissions for indoor use. It could be acrylics or phenolic resins such as phenol formaldehydes.
- Use water-based urethane finishes on wooden floors.
- Use par ticleboard made with phenol-formaldehyde resin rather than urea formaldehyde, to control indoor VOC emissions.
- Avoid the use of products using asbestos and CFC .
- Incorrosive atmospheres, metallic surfaces, and foundation reinforcements should be treated with suitable anti-corrosive treatments, such as epoxy, polyurethane coatings, etc.
- Minimise the use of metallic surfaces and metallic pipes, fitting, and fixtures.
- Use products and materials with reduced packaging and/or encourage manufacturers to reuse or recycle their original packaging materials.

Strategy for
sustainable use of energy

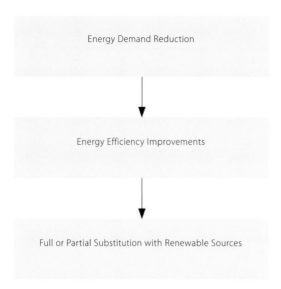

4. Sustainable Use of Energy

The primary function of a building envelope is to protect its occupants from heat, cold, rain, and to provide thermal and visual comfor t for work and leisure. In order to achieve comfort conditions, it is almost always essential to provide energy-consuming space conditioning and lighting devices.

Due to the long lives of the structures being built, the operating phase will consume the largest proportion of the energy resources compared to the overall life cycle. (UNEP-IETC, 2004). Therefore optimising the use of energy is crucial to reach the goal of a sustainable building. An eco-building should have an optimum energy performance and yet provide the desirable thermal and visual comfort. The energy usage of a building can be improved by: a) energy demand reduction; b) energy efficiency; c) use of renewable sources of energy.

4.1 Reduction in Energy Demand
To reduce energy demand, we need to reduce cooling/heating load and lighting load. The cooling/heating loads of a building are from various sources.

4.1.1 Building Form
• The compactness of a building could be measured by the ratio of surface area to volume(S/V ratio). The S/V ratio should be as low as possible in hot-dry and cold-dry climates, to minimise the rate of heat transfer. For hot, humid, tropical climate, the main aim should be to have a higher air flow inside the building, for which a low S/V ratio is not essential. (Krishan, A. et al., 2001)
• The perimeter to area ratio should be kept to the minimum, to reduce heat gains.
• The roof gets the maximum amount of direct solar radiation and hence its shape is important. As shown in next page, the higher the roof angle, the lesser the amount of direct radiation.

Cooling Load

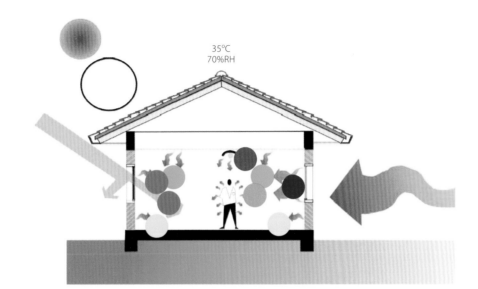

- Cooling load from roof
- Cooling load from envelope
- Cooling load from glazing
- Cooling load from infiltration
- Cooling load from equipment
- Cooling load from humans

35°C
70%RH

The Impace of Roof Angle

Direct Radiation

Direct Radiation

Direct Radiation

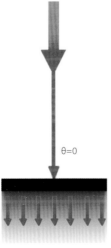

$\theta=0$

$\theta=15$

$\theta=45$

Q1=direct radiation × α

Q2=direct radiation × Cos15 × α

Q3=direct radiation × Cos45 × α

The Impace of Roof Angle

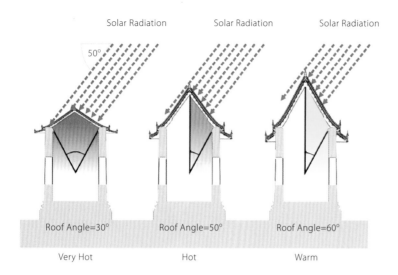

4.1.2 Landscaping
The figures in next page shows how proper landscaping, could reduce the ambient temperature and thereby the cooling load of the house. The first figure shows the conventional design and the second one, the design that has made use of landscaping.

4.1.3 Insulation
• Proper insulation is essential for avoiding heat gain (for interior cooling) and heat loss (for interior heating). For air conditioned buildings, apply insulation of high insulating capacity (low U-value) throughout the building. The insulation has to be on the hotter side, i.e., on the outside for interiors being cooled and on the inside for interiors being heated up.
• For buildings that are not air conditioned, do not use thermal insulation on the walls. This would trap heat inside the building. Use insulation only for the roofs exposed to direct solar radiation (UNEP-IETC, 2004, p.53)
• External wall with high thermal resistance is recommended to minimise the heat flow from external surfaces warmed by the sun.
• Wall insulation should be considered in the event of a building being air-conditioned. Some commonly used wall insulation types like mineral wool slabs, expanded/extruded polystyrene, aerated concrete blocks, etc. could be used for this purpose.
• The roof should be protected against excessive heat gain by appropriate insulation. Bonded mineral wool could be used for under deck roof insulation. Resin-bonded mineral wool is available in the form of slabs and rolls. These materials are available with or without lamination of aluminium foil. In India, the cost of mineral wool insulation (material only, for 50mm thick and 48kg/m³) is approximately $3/m² (excluding taxes). The cost of application with accessories is extra.
• Instead of roof insulation, a roof garden on the exposed roof area or a shaded roof would help to reduce heat ingress.

Effect of Climate and
Micro-Climate on
Cooling Load

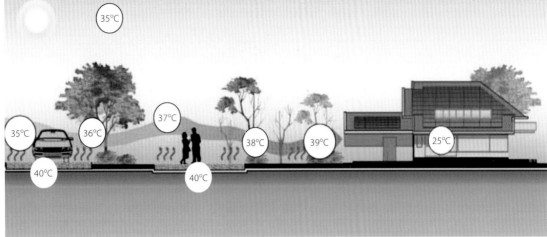

Effect of Micro-climate
Modification on
Cooling load

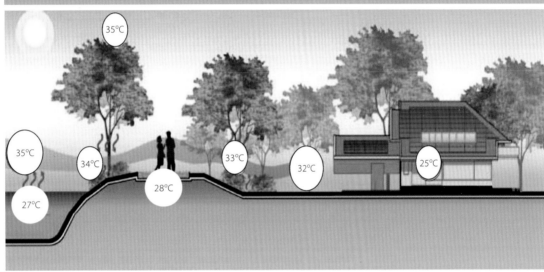

Thermal Resistance
Value(R) for
Insulation Materials

.

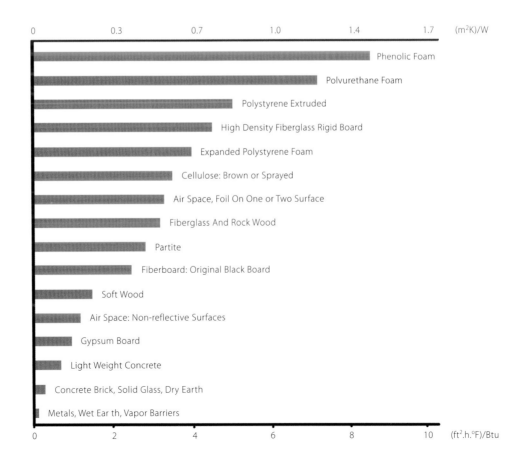

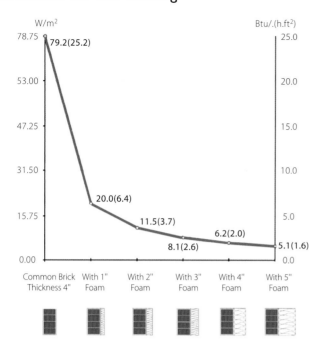

Heat Flow Through Insulation

4.1.4 Thermal Mass

• Due to the climate characteristics of warm-wet region, with small diurnal temperature range, the heat capacity of buildings should be as low as possible. This will avoid accumulation of heat in the day time and its subsequent release in the night time.

• Light-weight tiles with low heat capacity are preferred for the roofs, but it might cause heat stress during daytime.

• Furniture's should be as light as possible, to reduce their potential to store heat.

4.1.5 Natural Ventilation

Ventilation is required for fresh air, cooling for comfort conditions and for taking away the heat stored in the building structure. Fresh air is required for providing sufficient oxygen, diluting odours and to dilute CO_2 and pollutants inside the building.

For the successful design of a naturally ventilated building the wind characteristics and air flow patterns around a building, influenced by climate, neighbouring topography, plants and buildings has to be taken into account. Furthermore the fulfilment of natural ventilation depends on the location of vents (e.g. windows and roof lights) and the interior design (e.g. walls, openings and cour tyards).

Box 3: Natural Ventilation

(Roaf, S C., 2003)

Natural ventilation can be of two types. One is caused by wind pressure and the impact would depend on wind direction, speed and building shape. Using this we can provide single sided or cross ventilation. The other is caused by the density difference of air, caused by the difference in temperature between inside (warmer) and outside air. This is also called the "stack effect". If the inside air is colder, then a reverse stack effect can also be produced, which will bring in warm air from outside. See the figure (Facing above).

Dry Bulb Temperature	Relative Humidity (%)						
	30	40	50	60	70	80	90
°C	(Wind Speed, m/s)						
28	*	*	*	*	*	*	*
29	*	*	*	*	*	0.06	0.19
30	*	*	*	0.06	0.24	0.53	0.85
31	*	0.06	0.24	0.53	1.04	1.47	2.10
32	0.20	0.46	0.94	1.59	2.26	3.04	+
33	0.77	1.36	2.12	3.00	+	+	+
34	1.85	2.72	+	+	+	+	+
35	3.20	+	+	+	+	+	+

Desirable Wind Speeds For Thermal Comfort Conditions (Bis, 1987)

* None; + Higher than those acceptable in practice

• A building need not necessarily be oriented perpendicular to the prevailing outdoor wind. It may be oriented at any convenient angle between 0~30 degrees without losing any beneficial aspect of the breeze. If the prevailing wind is from east or west, the building can be oriented at 35 degrees to the incident wind so as to diminish the solar heat sacrificing slightly the reduction in air motion indoors.

• Large openings, doors, and windows are of advantage in a warm-wet climate provided they are effectively protected from penetration of solar radiation, rain, and intrusion of insects.

• Inlet openings in buildings should be well-distributed and should be located on the wind-ward side at a low level. Outlet openings should be located on the leeward side. Inlet and outlet openings at a high level would only clear the air at that level without producing air movement at the level of occupancy.

• Maximum air movement at a particular plane is achieved by keeping the sill height of the opening at 85% of the critical height (such as head level). The following levels are recommended according to the type of occupancy.

> For sitting on chair = 0.75m
> For sitting on bed = 0.60m
> For sitting on floor = 0.40m

• Inlet openings should not be obstructed by adjoining buildings, trees, signboards or other obstructions, or by partitions in the path of air flow.

• To maximise air flows, the inlet and outlet should not be in a straight line.

• For rooms having identical windows on opposite walls, the average indoor air speed increases rapidly by increasing the width of window by up to two-thirds of the wall width. Beyond that the increase in indoor air speed is in much smaller proportion, compared to the increase in window width. The air motion in the working zone is highest when the window height is 1.1m. A further increase in window height promotes air motion at a higher level of the window but does not contribute additional benefits as regards air motion in the occupancy zones in buildings.

• Greatest flow per unit area of openings is obtained by using the inlet and outlet openings of nearly equal areas at the same level.

• For a total area of openings (inlet and outlet) of 20-30 % of floor area, the average indoor wind velocity is about 30% of the outdoor velocity. Further increase in the window size, increases the available velocity but not in the same proportion. In fact, even under most favourable conditions, the maximum average indoor wind speed does not exceed 40% of the outdoor velocity.

• Where the direction of wind is quite constant and dependable and the size of the inlet should be kept within 30-50 % of the total area of openings. Where the direction of the wind is quite variable, the openings may be arranged equally on all sides, to the extent possible. Thus, no matter what the wind direction may be, effective air movement through the building would be assured.

• Windows of living rooms should open directly to an open space. In places where this is not possible, open space could be created in buildings by providing adequate courtyards.

• In case of rooms with only one wall exposed to the outside, provision of two windows on that wall is preferred to that of a single window.

• Windows located diagonally opposite each other with the windward window near the upstream corner gives better performance than other window arrangements for most building orientations.

• A single-side window opening can ventilate a space up to a depth of 6-7m. With cross-ventilation, a depth up to 15m may be naturally ventilated. Integration with an atrium or chimney to increase the "stack effect" can also ventilate deeper plan spaces.

• Horizontal louver, a sunshade atop a window, deflects the incident wind upwards and reduces air motion in the zone of occupancy. A horizontal slot between the wall and horizontal louver prevents upwards deflection of air in the interior of rooms. Provision of an inver ted L-type louver increases the room air motion provided that the vertical projection does not obstruct the incident wind.

• Provision of horizontal sashes, inclined at an angle of 45 degrees in an appropriate direction, helps promote indoor air motion. Sashes projecting outwards are more effective than those projecting inwards.

• Air motion at working plane, 0.4m above the floor, can be enhanced by 30% by using a pelmet-type wind deflector.

• Roof overhangs help promote air motion in the working zone inside buildings.

• A veranda open on three sides is to be preferred as it increases room air motion with respect to the outdoor wind, for most orientations of the building.

• A par tition placed parallel to the incident wind has little influence on the pattern of air flow, but when it is located perpendicular to the main flow, the same partition creates a wind shadow. In such cases, a par tition with a gap of 0.3m underneath helps augment air motion near the floor level in the leeward compar tment of the building.

• In a building unit having windows tangential to the incident wind, air movement increases when another unit is located at an end-on position on the downstream side.

• Air motion in two wings oriented parallel to the prevailing breeze is promoted by connecting them with a block in the downstream side.

• Air motion in a building is not affected by constructing another building of equal or smaller height on the leeward side, but it is slightly reduced if the building on the leeward side is taller than the windward block.

• Air motion in a shielded building is less than that in an unobstructed building. To minimize the shielding effect, the distance between the two rows should be 8H (8 times the height) for semi-detached houses and 10H for long row houses. However, for smaller spacing, the shielding effect is diminished by raising the height of the shielded building.

• The ventilation indoors can be improved by constructing buildings on earth mound, having a slant surface with a slope of 10 degrees on the upstream side.

• Roof overhangs and pitch should be as high as possible, to increase pressure difference and thereby the air flow.

• Provide openings in roof tiles, this would enhance stack effect and enable hot air to escape outside. One such example is the kindergarten for Sri Aurobindo International Institute of Educational Research in the warm and humid climate of Pondicherry, India, which has used specially designed roof tiles for escape of hot air.

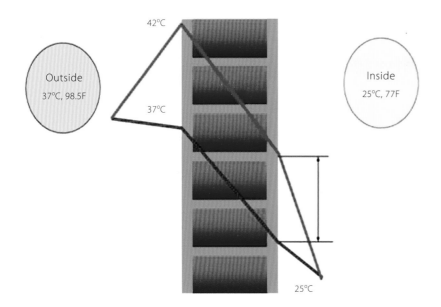

▬▬▬ With overhang

▬▬▬ 37°C Without overhang

• Provision should be made for forced ventilation strategies by use of ceiling/wall-mounted fans, exhaust fans.
• Provide buffer spaces like staircases, lifts, store, toilets, double-wallwithout opening etc., on at least 50% of the west wall
• Hedges and shrubs deflect air away from the inlet openings and cause a reduction in the indoor air motion.These elements should not be planted up to a distance of about 8m from the building because the induced air motion is reduced to a minimum in that case. However, air motion in the leeward par t of the building can be enhanced by planting low hedges at a distance of 2m from the building.
• Raising the building on stilts, at least 30cm above ground, has three main advantages in warm and wet climates. Fir st, it enables better ventilation by locating windows above the surrounding zone comprising lower buildings. Second, it enables cooling of the floor from below. Third, it helps to prevent moisture problems. It also gives flood protection, in flood prone areas.

4.1.6 Shading and Glazing
• In hot climates, shading should be provided for the east and west façade, to reduce solar heat gains especially during the morning and afternoon hours. Moveable blinds or curtains needs to be used carefully, since they impede ventilation, which is desirable in warm, humid climates. Overhangs and louvers provide effective shading. Similar shading can be provided by porticos. An example of the difference made to the heat gain, by providing a fixed overhang is shown in the figure above.

Shading Types (Baker, N., 2001)

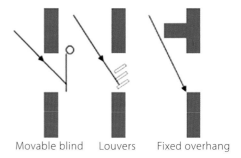

Movable blind   Louvers   Fixed overhang

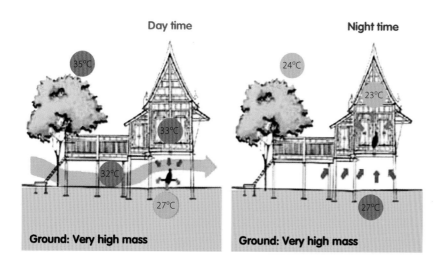

Day time   **Night time**

35°C   24°C

33°C   23°C

32°C

27°C   27°C

Ground: Very high mass   **Ground: Very high mass**

Trees with large foliage mass having trunks bare of branches up to the top level of the window, deflect the outdoor wind downwards and promote air motion in the leeward portion of buildings

• Minimise use of glass in buildings. Glass should not cover more than 50% of the wall area.

• Efficient glazing systems that maximise day-lighting and providing sun control should be adopted. The different types of glazing materials are: transparent glass, double glazing, absorbing glass, dark glass, reflective glass, polycarbonate, double poly carbonate with air space, corrugated fibre glass and acr ylic sheets. The properties of these glazing materials are given (Etzion, Y., 2001, p.119-120). See page 50.

4.1.7 External colours and textures

• For warm humid climates, light colour s and rough textures are preferred. Light colours are more reflective. Rough textures cause self shading and also increase the surface area for re-radiation. Both these factors help reduce heat gain.

• Thermal barrier paints could be used for the roof: These coatings form a seamless membrane that bridges hairline cracks. They have high reflectance, high emittance as well as a ver y low conductivity value. The approximate cost of application of thermal barrier paint in India is about USD 24/m^2.

4.1.8 Lighting

• The roof could be used as a day light source, along with some shading to reduce the heat gain.

• High windows provide the best distribution of light, but they should have baffles to avoid glare. Low windows allow in ground reflected light. From the point of view of light distribution, windows in the middle are least preferred.

• The penetration of daylight deep into the rooms can be increased by using light directing elements such as light shelves, reflective blinds, adjustable or fixed louvers or prismatic components in the window area, especially in the higher part. This could direct sufficient natural lighting up to 7m away from the windows. They act as shading elements and help to redirect the incoming light to the rooms´ ceiling. Their surfaces and that of the interior ceilings should have highly reflective surfaces (UNEP-IETC, 2004, p.73-74)

Properties of Glazing Materials (Etzion, Y., 2001, based on Watson, D. & Labs, K, 1983. Climatic Design-Energy Efficient Building Principles and Practices. Mcgraw-Hill Book Company, New York, P.188)

	Glass Thickness (mm)	Light Penetration (%)	Total Solar Radiation (%)
Glass			
Single, transparent	3	90	83
	3	88	77
Double, transparent	3	82	71
	3	78	60
Absorbent	3	84	65
	3	76	48
Dark	3	62	63
	3	42	44
Reflective/mirrore	-	8~34	11~37
Polycarbonates			
Single	3	86	89
	5	82	86
Double	-	73~80	21~60
Corrugated Fibre Glass			
Absolutely transparent		93	82
Translucent		87	81
White		32~66	21~60
Acrylic sheets			
Transparent		83	83
White		23~70	19~67

• The right type of glazing need to be chosen, for maximising day lighting and minimising solar heat gain, as mentioned earlier.
• The reflectance of internal finishes should be as per the desired daylight conditions.
• Avoid excessive illumination levels inside, which will add to the cooling load inside the building.
• Hard, smooth paving reflect light, causing glare. So they should be minimised. In case they are necessary, the surface could be made rough.

4.2 Energy Efficiency
Maximizing the energy efficiency of the building system offers fur ther oppor tunity for energy savings. Use of efficient energy consuming equipments for lighting, airconditioning, heating etc., can reduce the energy use in a building by at least 10-20%.

The main energy consuming equipments in buildings are the HVAC, and lighting systems. The efficiencies of these systems could vary depending on the technology used and the way they are operated and maintained. While implementing energy efficiency, care should be taken that it does not lead to a decrease in the quality of life. For example, it should not lead to reduced ventilation and higher concentrations of pollutants inside the house. Care should also be to avoid the rebound effect: for example, a tendency to increase the hours of usage of energy efficient equipment. This would cancel out the benefits from energy efficiency. Energy efficiency measures would also fail due to shortcomings in design, commissioning or use.

Following are some guidelines for minimising energy consumption in buildings and homes.
• Use high efficiency window air conditioners. Window air-conditioning systems are now available with some energy-saving features, such as sleep mode and filter-clean reminder. The sleep mode feature helps to save electric energy by increasing the set temperature, when the occupants are sleeping. The single-biggest reason

for inefficiency in window air conditioners is a dirty filter. A clogged filter results in increased power consumption and poor cooling. The filter-clean reminder feature reminds the user, when the filter is to be cleaned.

• Water cooled AC systems should be preferred over air cooled systems. Water-cooled units are of higher capacity and more energyefficient compared to air-cooled units. Air-cooled units are more suitable for places where water is scarce or of hard quality or where there is no space for installing a cooling tower.

• In all HVAC systems the, scaling or soiling of the heat transfer surfaces (condenser, cooling tower and evaporator) would reduce the system efficiency. Hence it is important to have proper maintenance practices.

• Shading the exposed part of the AC system would help to reduce up to 10 % of the power consumed by the compressor.

• Use fluorescent/ compact fluorescent lamps operating on electronic or low-loss ballast, for indoor lighting.

• Use HID (high-intensity discharge) lamps with minimum circuit efficacy of 80 lm/W for outdoor lighting, e.g., high-pressure sodium vapour lamps.

• Apply control devices judiciously, such as timers, photocells or occupancy sensors, to turn lights on and off.

• Provide fixed/pre-wired luminaires with sockets that will on ly accept lamps with high efficacy.

• Use energy efficient cooking stoves. They reduce energy consumption and indoor air pollution.

• Microwave ovens reduce energy use considerably, especially when cooking small quantities.

• In general, try to use the smallest size utensil for cooking. Cooking small quantities in a large utensil is inefficient.

• A pressure-cooker reduces cooking time and energy use considerably

• If possible, the size of the utensil on a stove should be larger than the size of the burner or the electric element. Otherwise there will be energy loss.

• An efficient burner will give a blue flame, instead of a yellow flame. This would depend on the cleanliness of the burner and the correct fuel to air ratio. Check for the efficiency of the gas burner, periodically.

• Electric stoves will continue radiating heat for a short period, even after it is turned off. Use this feature to save energy.

• Defrost frozen foods before cooking.

• Apart from spoiling the taste and reducing nutritional value, overcooking wastes energy.

• Certain foods that take long time to cook, like lentils, could be soaked in water, prior to cooking.

• Wherever it is feasible, substitute solid fuels with gaseous fuels, both for cooking and heating. Gaseous fuels are more efficient and cleaner than solid fuels. Replace electricity with gaseous fuels, wherever electricity is costly and/or is generated from polluting fuels.

4.3 Renewable Energy

Fossil fuels supply 80 percent of the world's primary energy at present, but resource depletion and long term environmental impacts might curb their use in future. Use of renewable forms of energy, based on solar, wind, and biomass energy helps in reducing demand for polluting, conventional fossil fuel based energy. The most likely application of renewable energy in the residential sector would be based on solar, wind or biomass energy. Before installing renewable technologies, check for all possibilities for energy demand reduction and energy efficiency. This would reduce the initial investment considerably.

5. Water and Sanitation

Detailed guidelines and resources on water and sanitation are available from WHO at http://www.who.int/water_sanitation_health. A brief overview of some aspects is given below.

5.1 Water Supply and Use

Considering the increasing demand and limited availability of water, it is impor tant that it be used and managed efficiently. In efficiently managing its water resources, most countries in Asia lag behind the developed countries and a lot could be done to improve the situation. To illustrate the potential, we could compare the water usage in India and in the US. In India, conventional toilets use 13.5 litres water per flush. The Energy Policy Act of USA, 1992, established standards that require new toilets to have a flow rate of 6.2 litres/flush, urinals with a flow rate of 3.8 litres/flush, and showerheads and lavatory and kitchen faucets with a flow rate of 9.5 litres/flush.

Some guidelines for the effective management of water are:
• Prepare a water balance for the site .
• Fix norms for water quality from various sources as per the specified local standards for different applications.
• Supplement surface water and ground water sources with rain water, by rain water harvesting.
• Use efficient fixtures that distribute of water at the desired pressure and avoid wastage and losses.
• Ensure regular monitor ing of both consumption patter ns and quality.
• Perform regular checks on plumbing systems to check for leakages, wastages, and system degradation.
• Adopt planting of native species and trees with minimal water requirement.
• Use mulches and compost for improving moisture retention in soil.
• Encourage rainwater har vesting and storage/ recharge for capturing good quality water. This is particularly important for coastal areas where groundwater is saline and intrusion of sea water has occurred.
• When water is sprayed on concrete str uctures for curing, free flow of water should not be allowed. Concrete structures should be covered with thick clothe/ gunny bags and water should be sprayed on them, which would avoid water rebound and will ensure sustained and complete curing. Ponds should be made using cement

and sand mortar to avoid water flowing away from the flat surface while curing.
• Concrete building blocks should be cured in shade .

Box 4: Sources of Water

Rain water could be collected by rain water har vesting. It provides good quality water and is a good way to supplement other sources of water. Surface water refers to the water from lakes, rivers and similar sources. They are easy to access, but are susceptible to pollution and hence needs to be treated and protected.Groundwater refers to the water available underground in aquifers, accessed by wells or boreholes. They could become polluted due to higher levels of chemicals such as arsenic, chlorides, fluorides etc.In humid regions, there is the possibility to extract water vapour in the atmosphere. For example, Professor Soontorn Boonyatikarn and his group at the Department of Architecture, Chulalongkorn University, Thailand has demonstrated a simple technique to collect around 40 litres of water per day from the atmosphere on a 125m² roof. It is based on the fact that a sloped roof is cooler than a flat roof and coating it with a low emissivity material could help to further reduce its temperature. At night time, the low temperature around the roof helps in condensing the water vapour in the atmosphere.

5.2 Sustainable Drainage

Conventional drainage methods usually involve transpor ting water as fast as possible to a drainage point, either by storm water drainage or a sewer. Sustainable drainage systems work to slow down the accumulation and flow of water into these drainage points and increases on-site infiltrations. This results in a more stable ecosystem as the water level and the water flow speed in the watercourse is more stable, and hence less erosion will take place.

The best strategy should be to slow down the drainage and then clean it by a natural system, before discharging it to a water course.

Run-off Coefficient for Various Surfaces	
Surface Type	Run-off Coefficient
Roofs Conventional	0.7~0.95
Concrete/Kota paving	0.95
Gravel	0.75
Brick Paving	0.85
Vegetation	
1%~3%	0.2
3%~10%	0.25
>10%	0.3
Turf Slopers	
0%~1%	0.25
1%~3%	0.35
3%~10%	0.4
>10%	0.45

• Drainage can be slowed down using swales, soak-ways, holding ponds and by having more pervious surfaces

• Pervious surfaces needs to be encouraged on site in the form of pavements and parking, which allow rainwater to seep through them.

Table 1 gives the typical values for the run-off coefficients for different types of surfaces. Pervious surfaces such as gravel or other open-textured material are only suitable for pedestrian or low-volume, lightweight traffic, such as walkways and personal driveways, but they are very easy to implement and inexpensive compared to the other methods. A combination of different types of pervious surfaces such as large or small paving blocks should be used. Large blocks have large holes that are filled with soil, and allow grass to grow in them. The surface is only suitable for foot traffic or occasional cars but has an aesthetic benefit due to the mostly grassy surface. Small blocks are impervious blocks that fit together in such a way so as to leave small openings in the joints between the blocks, allowing water to flow through. These blocks can take more and heavier traffic than large element blocks.

• Well planned roadways, par king lots, or walkways, with compact circulation patterns, could minimize pavement costs, centralize run-off, and improve efficiency of movement. This would help to reduce the ratio of impermeable surfaces to the gross site area.

• Restrict the net run-off from a site to a maximum of 60 %. In case the site hydrogeology does not allow the run-off factor to be 0.6, measures are to be taken to allow the collection of run-off into soak pits or collection pits so that the net run-off from the site is not more than 60 %.

• Make spill prevention and control plan that clearly states measures to stop the source of the spill, contain the spill, dispose the contaminated material, and provide training of personnel. Some of the hazardous wastes to be cautious about are pesticides, paints, cleaners, and petroleum products.

• The run-off from construction areas and material storage sites should be collected or diver ted so that pollutants do not mix with storm water runoff from

**Sources of household wastewater
(UNEP-IETC, 2000):**
1. Household
2. Storm water
3. Toilet
4. kitchen sink
5. dish wash
6. bath shower
7. cloth wash
8. misc.
9. black water
10. grey water
11. waste water
12. combined sewage

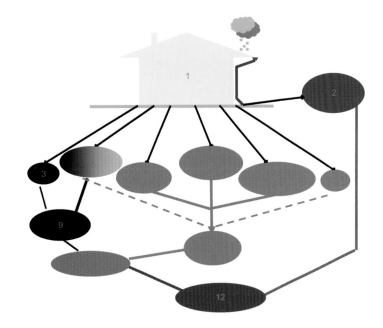

undisturbed areas. Temporary drainage channels, perimeter dike/swale, etc. should be constructed to carry the polluted water directly to municipal drains. The plan should indicate how the above is accomplished on site well in advance of the commencement of construction activity.

5.3 Waste Water treatment and Sanitation

Wastewater can be divided into greywater and blackwater. Greywater consists of the wastewater from washing/bathing, washing of clothes and from the kitchen. The wastewater from the toilet is called blackwater. Storm water also contains solids and pollutants, picked up from the surfaces it flows on. So it too requires treatment.

Stormwater collection is important from the point of view of flood control. If wastewater is combined with storm water, we call it a combined sewage. The main aim of waste water treatment is to reduce the Biological Oxygen Demand (BOD) and Suspended Solids (SS) to acceptable levels. Normally BOD is reduced to less than 20 mg/L, and SS to less than 30 mg/L. SS is removed by filtration and sedimentation. BOD is mainly removed by aerating the water, but nowadays anaerobic treatment is also being done, mainly to recover energy. If the waste water is discharged to water bodies that are sensitive to nutrients, then nutrients also should be removed. (UNEP-IETC, 2000)

Pathogenic and faecal indicator micro-organisms needs to be reduced to acceptable levels, to ensure that this will not pose any threat to human health, Different types of treatment techniques can be adopted depending on land availability and on the quantity, and characteristics of waste water. Removing BOD and SS produces sludge. The sludge has to be fur ther treated, before reuse or disposal. Treatment plants, which are used for treating sewage, are usually based on the biological process. The process is dependent on natural micro-organisms that utilize oxygen and organic contaminants in waste water to generate CO_2, sludge, and treated water.

**The Inverted Waster Pyramid
(UNEP-IETC, 2003b)**

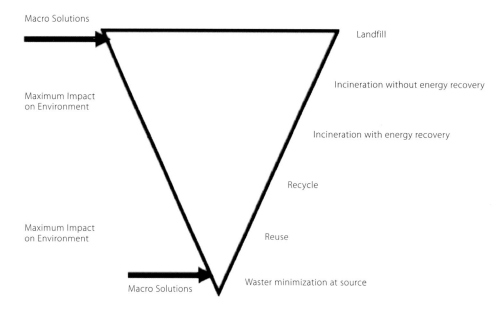

Macro Solutions

Landfill

Incineration without energy recovery

Incineration with energy recovery

Maximum Impact
on Environment

Recycle

Maximum Impact
on Environment

Reuse

Macro Solutions

Waster minimization at source

The guidelines that could be followed are:
• Do not mix up different kinds of wastes. Collect solid wastes, waste water and storm water separately, but have an integrated plan to deal with them.
• Promote low-cost decentralised waste water treatment system.
• Develop norms based on existing standards for reuse of treated water for non-potable applications.
• Water under or near a pit or septic tank can get polluted. To prevent this, septic tanks should be located 15-20m away from the nearest water supply point and 3m from the nearest house.
• The kitchen should be separated from animals and the toilet, to ensure hygiene.

6. Solid Waste Management

Solid waste generated from buildings consists of a mix of biodegradable, nonbiodegradable, and inert waste. Municipal solid waste is usually dumped in landfill sites or open dump sites, leading to air and water pollution. Through efficient waste management methods, a significant amount of solid waste could be reduced, recycled or reused. (SKAT, 2001,2002).

Traditionally urban solid wastes are managed in a hierarchy that looks like an inverted pyramid as shown below. Innovative solutions have been applied for each level of this hierarchy, for reducing environmental impacts, such as material and energy recovery, waste water management etc. The technical inputs required increases towards the top of the pyramid. The degree of partnership required decreases towards the upper level. (UNEP-IETC , 2003b)

The guidelines are as follows:
• Provide facilities for collection of segregated waste at the household and colony levels.
• Identify facilities for recycling of non-biodegradable wastes such as plastics, glass, and paper.

• Develop decentralised treatment and resource recovery systems at site based on composting or anaerobic digestion process for segregated organic waste. Identify appropriate options for the use of biogas and manure.

• For good perfor mance, resource recover y processes like biomethanation and composting should be given proper care, like in any production process. Marketing and the quality of the product, should be given due importance.

• In most countries in Asia, open dumping is practiced. Develop norms for disposal of non-degradable and iner t waste in landfills based on local standards, to ensure safe environment in the surrounding areas. Sanitary landfills needs to be designed and people need to be trained in managing and maintaining it.

• A common mistake is to provide the infrastructure, but neglect the managerial aspects. It usually involves managing a large workforce, working together closely with the public and handling teething financial and maintenance problems.

• Establish an efficient waste reduction, recycling, and reuse (3R) programme.

• Avoid or reduce toxic and hazardous materials. Recycle items such as ballasts, mercury-based lighting products, used oil, unusable batteries, etc.

• Reuse construction debris. In isolated areas that do not have indigenous manufacturing units for building materials, like the islands in Maldives, building materials have to be imported. Optimisation of building materials becomes a priority in these areas. In such cases, the use of construction debris after segregation and crushing could be considered. This is also true for many of the disaster affected areas.

• Recycling and reuse can be enabled if easy disassembling of the building and its components is possible. The following are principles of design for disassembly (DfD) as applied to buildings (Kiber t, C J., 2003)

- Minimise the number of types of materials & components
- Avoid composite materials and make inseparable products from the same material

- Avoid secondary finishes to materials
- Provide standard and permanent identification of material types and components
- Use mechanical rather than chemical connections.
- Minimise numbers of fasteners and connectors. Minimise types of connectors
- Use an open building system with interchangeab le parts
- Use modular design
- Separate the structure from the cladding
- Provide access to all building components
- Design components sized to suit handling at all stages
- Provide adequate tolerance to allow for disassembly
- Design joints and connectors to withstand repeated assembly and disassembly
- Allow for parallel disassembly
- Use prefabricated sub-assemblies
- Use lightweight materials and components

Box 5: Site specific factors to be considered for solid waste management
Composition of the waste: This would impact handling and transportation options as well as options for recycling, reusing, recovering energy or incineration. For example, if the moisture content of the waste is high, incineration would not be possible.
Accessibility to waste collection points.
Costs of storage and transport.
Social attitudes to waste collection services such as willingness to segregate waste to assist recycling; willingness to pay for waste management services; opposition to siting of waste treatment and disposal facilities etc.

7. Indoor Environment Quality

People spend 80%–90% of their time indoors, at home, school, and work. Hence indoor environmental quality is an important parameter in a sustainable habitat. Poor indoor air quality causes headaches, tiredness, shortness of breath, and allergic reactions such as sinus congestion, irritation of the eyes and throat, sneezing, coughing, and wheezing. In some cases, an allergic reaction of the lungs (hypersensitivity pneumonitis) has also been reported. Indoor air quality is affected by ventilation rates, temperature and humidity, building materials, kind of devices used indoor and outdoor air pollution entering into the home.

Biological contaminants also contribute to the poor indoor air quality.In coastal regions, warm, humid conditions provide an excellent environment for breeding of dust mites, moulds, and fungi. The contaminants include animal dander, water-borne microbes, moulds, etc., all of which can cause an allergic reaction. Some organisms can contaminate water sources and become air-borne through humidifiers. Combustion by-products due to incomplete burning of fuels (oil, gas, kerosene, wood, coal, etc.) generate gases and tiny particles like carbon monoxide and respirable suspended par ticulate matter, nitrogen dioxide, formaldehyde, ammonia, etc., which are known to cause adverse health impacts.

Radon is a naturally occurring radioactive gas given off by traces of uranium in soil and rock. Some buildings could have high levels of radon in its str ucture, leading to an increase in the long-term risk of lung cancer. The guidelines for maintaining indoor environmental quality are as follows:
• Use interior finishes and products with zero VOC (volatile organic compound) or low VOC content.
• Indoor ventilation rate should be maintained as per ASHRAE 62.2- 2004. (ASHRAE, 2006) or national standards.
• Design for indoor ther mal comfort level as per ASHRAE 55-2004.
• Avoid use of hazardous mater ials e.g., asbestos.
• Keep the house clean and dust-free to reduce allergens such as house dust mites, pollen, and animal dander.
• Avoid leaving any material that could degrade/rot inside house.
• To prevent growth of mould, lower the humidity by venting moist areas or by installing dehumidifiers or humidistats.

- Disinfect the house regularly, especially whenever mould is seen to be growing.
- Separate cooking area from living area.
- Use high-efficiency combustion devices with outside vents (chimney).
- Implement no-smoking rules.
- Design for day lighting asper the local code.
- Provide views from all living spaces.
- Adopt measures to tackle noise pollution inside building, if there are high noise sources, such as airport in the vicinity. Use appropriate constructed or natural screens to reduce the impact of noise from external sources.
- Ensure proper slab construction between floors to deter structureborne noise.
- Choose internal surface finishes based on acoustic performance.
- Consider acoustic lining for noise-producing equipment e.g., dieselgenerating sets.
- Give sufficient ventilation to the kitchen.
- Use stoves that have chimney.

8. Construction Administration

Environmentally conscious construction practices can minimise site disturbance, construction waste and the use of natural resources. It also reduces the overall project cost. The guidelines are as follows:
- Incorporate environmental guidelines into the construction contract.
- Develop construction safety norms and include the same in contractor's document.
- Identify potential health hazards and formulate measures to address the same.
- Isolate construction sites from occupied areas.
- Adopt good practices for air pollution management on site.
- Optimise water use in constr uction by adopting water-efficient technologies e.g., use of ready mix concrete .
- Use recycled water for construction.
- Recycle and re-use construction debris

9. Building Commissioning, Operation And Maintenance

Commissioning involves examining, approving or withholding approval of the building and its sub-systems to ensure that it is constructed in accordance with the contract documents, and is performing as intended. Commissioning enables the integration and organisation of design, construction, operation, and maintenance of a building and its sub-systems.

The O&M (operation and maintenance) costs throughout the building life cycle are considerable and could exceed the buildings' initial investment. The design intent of a building and systems is not met unless it is maintained properly. Appropriate maintenance procedures also help to keep the building and its sub-systems in order, so that they give the same output as during the initial stages.

The guidelines are:
• Prepare a detailed commissioning plan. Prepare the criteria for processes and systems to be commissioned.
• Involve the design team in monitoring the commissioning process.
• Ensure commissioning is in accordance with the contr act document.
• Ensure that qualified professionals are engaged in operation and maintenance.
• Train facility staff for proper maintenance of facilities.
• Prepare a detailed O&M plan with written policies and procedures for inspection, preventive maintenance, repairs, and cleaning. Material safety data sheets and information on cleaning chemicals to be used for cleaning, frequencies of cleaning, and pest-control methods, should be properly documented and followed.
• Monitor the performance parameters of the buildings and compare it with established benchmarks.
• Monitor thermal and visual comfort parameters.

A Scan of Eco-Housing Technologies and Techniques

A brief scan of some of the technologies and techniques that could be useful for implementing the eco-housing guidelines is given below.

1. Site Preparation

1.1 Mulching

Mulching is one of the simplest and most-beneficial practices used in landscaping. Mulch is simply a protective layer of a material that is spread on top of soil. Mulches can either be organic, such as grass-clippings, straw, bark chips, and similar materials, or inorganic, such as stones, brick chips, and plastic. Both, organic and inorganic mulches have numerous benefits, such as: protect soil from erosion; reduce compaction from impact of heavy rains; conserve moisture, reducing the need for frequent waterings; maintain a more even soil temperature; prevent weed growth; keep fruits and vegetables clean; keep feet clean, allowing access to the garden even when damp; and provide a "finished" look to the garden.

1.2 Phytoremediation

Phytoremediation involves the use of plants to remediate contaminated soils, sludge, sediments and water. It supplements, and in some cases replaces conventional mechanical clean-up technologies. It is mostly used for sites with low to medium contaminant concentrations, and contamination in shallow soils. (UNEP-IETC, 2003a)

2. Building Materials and Technologies

2.1 Prefabrication

Prefabrication of building components in factories is possible, like that of walls, floors, roofs, windows, doors etc. This helps to save time, labour costs and ensures better quality. Even if onsite construction is done, some prefabricated components like windows and doors could be used.

2.2 Compressed Earth Blocks(CEB)

CEB's are earthen bricks compressed with hand-operated or motorised hydraulic machines. To produce them, soil (raw or stabilised) is slightly moistened, poured into a steel press, and then compressed. The soil should be of good quality, and should not contain any organic material that can decompose. Stabilisers like cement, lime, or gypsum, ensure better compressive strength and water resistance.

The advantages of CEB's are: uniform sizes and shapes, use of locallyavailable materials and reduction of transportation; avoidance of wood in manufacturing; lower production cost and energy input compared with fired bricks.

2.3 Concrete Hollow Blocks
Concrete block construction are available in various sizes and shapes. Compared to fire clay bricks, their advantages are: better insulation proper ties; no fuel or wood required for production; voids can be used for filling with steel bars and concrete or with electrical installation and plumbing; lighter in weight; easy to use.

2.4 Vertical Shaft Brick Kiln Technology (VSBK) for Brick Production
It is an energy efficient and cleaner method of producing bricks, with 30 to 50 percent savings when compared with conventional methods. It consists of one or more rectangular, vertical shafts within a kiln structure.

At a time, one batch of dried green bricks is loaded at the top of the shaft, followed by the next batch. A weighed quantity of powdered coal is spread on each layer uniformly to fill the gaps. The layers of green bricks gradually pass through the shaft encountering pre-heating, firing and cooling zones before they reach the exit at the bottom. The brick unloading is done from the bottom using a trolley on rails. The kiln can be operated year long and the investment is low. Suspended Particulate Matter can be reduced up to 90%, while carbon dioxide emissions could be lowered by 30 to 50%. The bricks are 95% uniform and of high quality, unlike in conventional technologies where maintaining quality is difficult.

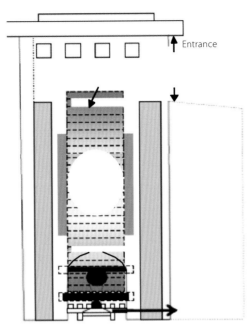

Entrance

Vertical Shaft Brick Kiln

2.5 Habitech Self-Contained Housing Delivery System

The Habitech building system has been developed by the Habitech Centre in the Asian Institute of Technology, Thailand. The components of the building system are prefabricated modular inter locking concrete-based elements that can be put in place easily without the need for heavy equipment. Because the components are self-aligning, unskilled workers can take part in the building process.

The production facility can be set up locally, creating jobs that generate income for local populations. A typical production facility will employ 30 to 40 workers in production and in construction for the project it supplies. Production facilities can become permanent and address local construction markets. The scale of the production process could range between 2 houses a week to 10 houses a day. By using this system, construction costs could be lowered by 30 to 50%.

3. Energy Management

3.1 Cogeneration

Cogeneration or combined heat and power (CHP) refers to the use of a single source of energy (fuel), to produce both power and heat. In contrast, a normal thermal power plant produces electricity only. This is normally a decentralised system, implemented at the end user side. A large improvement in efficiency of the overall system is possible due to the usage of the waste heat and the avoidance of the transmission and distribution losses, as compared to using grid power from a thermal power plant. The heart of the system is the equipment producing power and heat. This could be based on gas turbines, steam turbines, IC engines, fuel cells or a combination of them.

3.2 Energy Recovery Heat Exchangers

Indoor air can be 2 to 5 times more polluted than outdoor air. One of the reasons is that modern buildings have less ventilation and are much more sealed up for space conditioning and energy conservation objectives. For such spaces it is essential that there be a provisionfor leaking out the pollutant build up and the addition of fresh air. On the other hand, better ventilation will result in energy loss in air conditioned spaces. To avoid energy loss, an energy recovery heat exchanger is used. These heat exchangers allow the recovery of the cooling in the exhaust air, by transferring it to the incoming warmer fresh air and thus saving energy. The main modification required in the existing system is to reroute the fresh air and the exhaust air through the energy recovery heat exchanger.

They al so have the dual purpose of humidity control, due to condensation in the heat exchanger and/or by having desiccants that absorbs moisture from the incoming air. Once these desiccant materials are saturated with moisture, they could be regenerated by the incoming fresh air. By recovering energy, the heat exchanger adds to the cooling capacity of the HVAC system. Thus they reduce the need for a bigger air conditioning system, resulting in savings in the initial investment of new systems. The savings from such a system can be realised only in well insulated, air tight buildings.

3.3 Ground Cooling
At about 10-14 metres below the surface the soil has a constant temperature throughout the year, close to the mean annual outdoor air temperature. (Yannas, S., 2003) Hence during summers, it could be cooler than the outside air temperature and during winters it could be warmer. Ground cooling can be done by direct contact, by constructing the house par tially or completely underground.

The other method is by using earth to air heat exchanger pipes. For ear th to air heat exchangers, outside air is taken through pipes buried in the ground. The air is indirectly cooled by the surrounding soil. The air at the outlet of the exchanger is cooler than the outside temperature.

3.4 Movable Insulation

A movable insulation can protect the roof from the sun during the day but can be retracted at night to allow radiant cooling of the roof surface to the cool night sky. The cooling effect can be enhanced by the exposure and insulation of a large thermal storage mass, like a roof pond. The roof pond has to be covered with an insulating layer during the day and opened up for radiative cooling at night. (UNEP-IETC, 2004, p.90)

3.5 Vapour Absorption Refrigeration System

The vapour absorption refrigeration system uses heat as the main energy input, unlike the conventional vapour compression refrigeration systems using electricity for the compressors. The heat could be any form of waste heat or solar radiation. It runs on the principle that certain liquids (absorbent) have a strong tendency to absorb specific vapours (refrigerant). The refrigerant liquid which evaporates at low temperature absorbs heat from surrounding when it evaporates and thereby cools the surrounding. For airconditioning temperatures, pure water is used as the refrigerant and lithium bromide solution is used as the absorbent. Apart from reducing the use of electricity, it also helps to avoid ozone depleting refrigerants used in conventional systems. (UNEP-IETC, 2004, p.91)

3.6 High Efficiency Cooking Stoves

Higher efficiency cooking stoves use several techniques to reduce the fuel input and emissions. These include: fine tuning the air-fuel ratio to ensure complete combustion without loosing much heat in the flue gas; improved insulation; increasing the length of travel of the flue gas to improve the heat transfer; pre-heating the air before combustion; and sometimes using catalytic converters for ensuring complete combustion.

3.7 Electronic Ballasts

Chokes or ballasts are required for star ting and stabilising the illumination of

Fluorescent lights. Conventional ballasts are electromagnetic and have a higher loss of around 12 Watts. Electronic ballasts have a loss of 3 watts or less. Electronic ballasts also supply power to the lamp at a much higher frequency and this increases the efficiency and output from the lamp.

3.8 Compact Fluorescent Lamp (CFL)

They are smaller diameter, low power fluorescent lamps that are often used as an alternative to incandescent bulbs. They are much more efficient than incandescent lamps. For example, a 9 watt CFL can replace a 60 watt incandescent bulb. They also could last around 8 to 10 times longer.

3.9 High Intensity Discharge (HID) Lamp

The HID lamps have a longer life and provide more light (lumens) per watt than most other light sources. They are available as mercury vapour, metal-halide, high-pressure sodium, and low-pressure sodium types. They are mostly used outdoors.

3.10 Occupancy Sensors

It is a control device that senses the presence of a person in a given space, in order to control lighting and sometimes HVAC. They are mainly of three types: infrared, ultrasonic and acoustic sensors. Infrared sensors detect motion when someone (heat source) moves from one place to another. The sensor needs a direct line of sight to the occupants to detect motion; hence they are not ideal for spaces with partitions or with irregular shapes. They are comparatively less sensitive and hence chance for false triggering from small movements is less. Ultrasonic sensors emit high-frequency waves which bounce off objects in the room and return to the sensors. Objects moving in the space shift the frequency of the returning signals and this shift is detected by the sensors. They are very sensitive and do not require a direct line of sight to occupants. Hence there are chances for false signals like windblown cur tains or papers. Acoustic sensors rely on voices, machinery sounds, keyboard tapping and other typical daily noises. This technology works well in areas with par titions or obstructions.

Nowadays a combination of these technologies is used, to avoid false signals. For example, while an ultrasonic sensor would sense a wind blown paper and would tend to turn the lights on, the infrared sensor would not sense a movement of heat and would override the ultrasonic signal. Installation, commissioning and fine tuning of the system is critical to realise energy savings. (Santa Monica Green Building Programme)

3.11 Timers and Photosensors

Timers can be used to automatically turn on and off lights at specific times. For outdoor lighting, if we use a simple timer, then we have to reset it for the different seasons. In such case, it would be more convenient to use it in combination with other controls, like a photosensor. Photosensors senses the ambient lighting levels and accordingly controls the light output.

3.12 Dimmers

Dimmers are control devices used to reduce the lighting output.

3.13 Day Lighting Techniques

There are several methods by which artificial lighting can be reduced through enhancing day lighting. The techniques in vogue make use of specially designed openings, the optical properties of glazing materials, use of reflectors and the photometric characteristics of surfaces (texture, colour and transmissivity). The techniques can be classified into: openings on vertical walls; openings in the roof; atria; and light ducts. (UNEP-IETC, 2004)

4. Renewable Energy Technologies

4.1 Solar Photovoltaic (PV) Technologies

The solar PV (photovoltaic) technology comprises photovoltaic modules, which collect and conver t solar energy into electrical energy and the balance of systems (BOS) designed to store, and deliver the generated electricity. Balance of systems

A Grid Connected Solar PV System:
1. Solar panels
2. Inverter
3. Fuse box/meters
4. Power demand
5. Excess power exported to the grid
6. Additional power from the grid

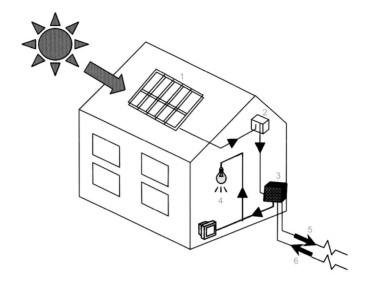

includes the support structure; wiring; batteries; power electronics and controls. The material commonly used for solar cell production is silicon – either crystalline (mono and poly) or amorphous silicon. Out of it, crystalline silicon cells are the most popular, though more expensive. Thin film solar modules are cheaper because less material is used and it has a relatively easier manufacturing process. wvIn spite of this, it still has a smaller market, mainly due to its relatively lower efficiency. Generation is possible only when the sun is shining, so a battery is needed to store electricity and use it at night or during periods of insufficient sunshine. In places where sale to the grid is possible and attractive, the user could avoid the use of batteries, by using the grid as the storage medium. An inverter is used to convert the DC current into AC current. The amount of sunlight and hence the output from the PV module varies according to the angle of the module relative to the position of the sun in the sky. At present, PV based power is more costly compared to that of grid electricity in most cases. However, in places with no access to the electric grid or with a high electricity cost, PV system is an attractive option. The PV module would have a life of 20 years or more, the inverter around 12 years and the battery around 3 to 5 years.

Building Integrated PV systems (BIPV)

PV arrays are normally mounted on special-suppor t structures. However, they can also be made an integral par t of the building envelope. There are several building elements that can readily accommodate PV, such as cur tain walls, atria, and roofs. In addition, new products are being developed with PV as an integral component, such as active shading elements, building glazing, or roof tiles. It can thus replace conventional building materials, in addition to being a power generation option.

Solar Home System (SHS)

It consists of a single PV module of 18–75 W capacity; a deep discharge-type lead acid battery; charge controller; 1, 2 or 3 CFLs (compact fluorescent lamps); and a DC power point for another appliance such as radio, tape recorder.

The module generates energy that is stored in the battery and can be used at any time of the day.

PV-based Mini-grids

A mini-grid refers to small power plants that supply three-phase AC electricity through low-tension distribution networks to households for domestic power, commercial (for example, shops, cycle repair shops, and flour mills) activities, and community requirements such as drinking water supply and street lighting. State-of-the-art batteries and inverters are used to ensure long life and reliable field performance. An appropriately designed mini-grid can easily supply power for 8–10 hours daily. Though there is no limit on the capacity of the mini-grid, PV-based mini-grids are typically of 25–100 kW. Installation, operation and maintenance of these mini-grids are normally contracted on a turnkey basis to the PV supplier. At the local level, the village community is expected to play a critical role in facilitating payment collection, monitoring of theft, complaint redress, etc.

Solar Street Lighting System

Street lighting is another application, which could utilise PV technology.
A typical system could have the following configuration:
- 74 W solar PV module
- 12 V, 75 Ah tubular plate battery with battery box
- Charge controller cum inverter
- 11-watt CFL lamp with fixtures
- 4 m mild steel lamp post above ground level

Solar Water Pumps

Pumping of water is an application, which does not require battery storage. In this system, PV modules are directly coupled to the motor-pump unit and water is pumped as long as the sun shines. There are several system designs based on various types of motor and pump sets. For example, the most commonly used ones in India are 900 or 1800 W DC surface and AC submersible motor-pump sets. These pumps are suitable for both drinking and irrigational requirement.

4.2 Solar Water Heating System

Solar energy could be used to heat water by using a solar water heating system, usually placed on the roof top. Water is passed through pipes in an absorber, which is placed in a glazed and well insulated collector. The water gets heated up and is then passed to an insulated storage tank. Thermo-siphon systems do not use pumps. The water flows by gravity and is based on thermodynamic principles. In forced circulation systems, a pump is used for water circulation. In most places, solar thermal systems are cost competitive with other modes of water heating. (UNEP-IETC, 2004, p.94)

4.3 Solar Stills

They use direct solar energy for desalting saline water. These devices generally imitate a part of the natural hydrological cycle in that the saline water is heated by the sun's rays so that production of water vapour increases. The water vapour is then condensed on a cool surface, and the condensate is collected as water. In a solar still plant, the only moving par t is the pump, used to pump saline water from the well. The solar still can desalt saline water having a wide range of salinity, including sea water. In addition, it also removes toxic ions and bacteriological contamination. Thus, solar stills are ideal to provide safe drinking water to isolated communities of small villages, islands, lighthouses, and salt works. The average yield of a 1 m^2 single slope, single basin, solar still is about 2 litres per day. The capital cost of a commercial solar still of 1 m^2 area is about USD 120.

Some preconditions for setting up solar stills of relatively larger sizes are as follows:
• Uninterrupted supply of saline water preferably over 10,000ppm and sunny weather throughout the year.

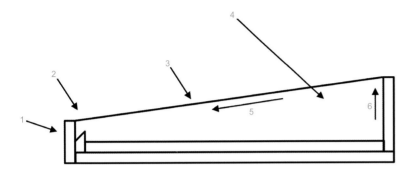

Solar Still:
1. Insultation
2. Trough
3. Glass
4. solar energy
5. Condensation
6. Evaporation

• The quality of the glass sealing plays a very crucial role as far as performance of still is concerned as vapour-leakage through the joints appreciably reduce the output.

4.4 Wind Energy

A wind turbine transforms the energy in the wind into mechanical power, which can then be used directly for work (pumping, grinding etc.) or for further conversion to electric power. The key factors that decide the suitability of a site for wind power and the kind of equipments are: how often the wind blows and at what speeds; how turbulent the wind is; and the wind direction.

4.5 Biomass

The use of biomass for energy is considered a carbon neutral activity, since it absorbs the same amount of carbon in growing as it releases when consumed as a fuel. Another advantage is that it can be used to generate heat or electricity with the same equipments that are now used with fossil fuels. Instead of burning the loose biomass fuel directly, it could also be used conveniently in a compacted form as briquettes. Biomass energy can also be used as bio-gas by an anaerobic digestion process. This is being widely promoted in rural areas as a source of energy for cooking, though it could have other applications like small scale power generation. The residue could be used as manure.

4.6 Mini or Micro Hydel Power

Hydro power is one of the cheapest, and cleanest sources of energy, though big dams result in many environmental and social problems. Smaller dams (mini or micro hydro power) are free from these problems and could be used for power generation in remote areas that have no access to the grid.

5. Water Supply and Use
5.1 Rainwater Harvesting

Rainwater Harvesting System:
1. Washout tap
2. Overflow
3. Downpipe
4. Guttering
5. Moveable pipe allows runoff from first spell of rain to drain away
6. Pre-filter
7. Outlet
8. Gravel soakway
9. Collection area - corrugated iron roof

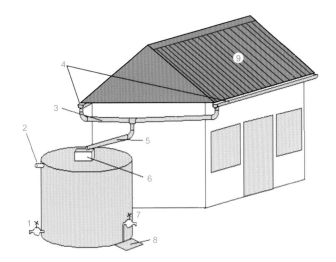

It is traditionally practised in many parts of Asia, e.g., in Maldives this is the only source of drinking water in many islands. PVC tanks are predominantly used for storing rainwater. The decision whether to store or recharge water depends on the rainfall pattern of a particular region. Maldives being a high rainfall zone, rain falls throughout the year, barring a few dry periods. In such a case, one can depend on storage tank as the period between two spells of rain is short. Rainwater drainage pipes collect rainwater from roof to storage container. Appropriate precautions should be taken to prevent contamination of stored water. Mesh filters provided at mouth of drain pipe prevent leaves and debris from entering the system. If stored water is to be used for drinking, a sand filter should also be provided. Underground masonry/reinforced cement concrete tanks, or over ground PVC tanks could be used for storage of rainwater. Each tank must have an overflow system connected to the drainage/recharge system.

Rainwater collected from rooftops is free of mineral pollutants like fluoride and calcium salt but is likely to be contaminated by air and surface pollutants. All these contaminations can be prevented largely by flushing off the first 10-20 minutes of rainfall. Water quality improves over time during storage in tank as impurities settle in the tank if water is not disturbed. Even pathogenic organisms gradually die out due to storage. Additionally, biological contamination can be removed by other means.

5.2 Plumbing Fixtures
• Low-flow flush toilets: Low-flush toilets have a flow rate of 6 litres/flush, while ultralow-flush toilets are available with a flow of 3.8 litres/flush.
• Low-Flow Urinals: Low-flow urinals consume water at the flow rate of 3.8 litres/flush. Use of an electronic flushing system or magic eye sensor can fur ther reduce the flow of water to 0.4 litres per flush.
• Waterless urinals: Waterless urinals use no water but a biodegradable liquid for cleaning. These functions by allowing the urine to pass though the biodegradable liquid

using a funnel system called car tridge thus preventing any odour and maintains a hygienic surrounding. The advantage of using such a system is not only saving water but also reducing the load in the sewer system. The average life of the car tridge is 7000 uses.

• Water taps: The use of conventional faucets results in flow rates as high as 20 lpm (litres per minute). Low-flow faucets are available which can result in withdrawal of water at a flow rate of 9.5 lpm. In addition to this, further reduction of water consumption is possible by using auto control valves, pressure-reducing device, aerators and pressure inhibitors for constant flow and magic eye solenoid valve selfoperating valves.

• Showerheads: Showers of different diameters at different pressures result in different flow rates. The conventional showerheads have a range of flow rates of 10-25 lpm. Fixtures are available with flow rates of 9.5 lpm.

5.3 Water Treatment Technologies

Water-borne diseases can be caused by microbiological contamination. Excessive levels of fluoride, nitrates, iron, and arsenic can cause severe health disorders. Water needs to be stored properly and treated to national or WHO (World Health Organisation) standards, before being used for drinking purpose.

5.3.1 Household Level Treatment

Some means of disinfecting water at household level are enumerated below:

• Boiling: Boiling is a very effective method of purification and very simple to carry out. Boiling water for 10 to 20 minutes is enough to remove all biological contaminants.

• Chemical disinfection using chlorine: Chlorination is done with stabilised bleaching powder (calcium hypo chlorite, $CaOCl_2$), which is a mixture of chlorine and lime. Chlorination can kill all types of bacteria and make water safe for drinking purposes. About 1gm (approximately ¼ tea spoon) of bleaching powder is sufficient to treat 200 litres of water. Sometimes chlorine tablets are used. They are easily available

commercially. One tablet of 0.5 g is enough to disinfect 20 litres of water.
• Filtration
- Charcoal water filter. A simple charcoal filter can be made in a drum or an earthen pot. The filter is made of gravel, sand and charcoal, all of which are easily available.
- Sand filter. Sand filters have commonly available sand as filter media.
They are easy and cheap to construct. These filters can be employed for treatment of water to effectively remove turbidity (suspended par ticles like silt and clay), colour, and micro-organisms.
- Ceramic filter. These filters are manufactured commercially on a wide scale. Most water purifiers available in the market are of this type.

5.3.2 Community Level Water Treatment

Other systems are available for various kinds of community applications. For example, an on-line dosing coagulant system could be used to prevent microbial growth in treated, stored water. Systems have been developed to treat brackish water, fluorides, arsenic, and iron. These are also available as hand pump attachments. The par ticles are either adsorbed on a resin or onto a catalytic media. Another option for providing quality water at low cost is to use "package plants." Package plants consist of various components of the treatment process, such as chemical feeders, mixers, flocculators, sedimentation basins, and filters in a compact assembly. As these units are assembled based on standard designs, they are cheaper as compared to those that are built on site.

6. Waste Water Treatment and Sanitation
6.1 Wastewater Treatment
Wastewater can be treated onsite or off-site. The common on-site treatment is done by
• Pit latrines and Pour flush latrines
• Composting toilets
• Septic tanks and Imhoff tanks

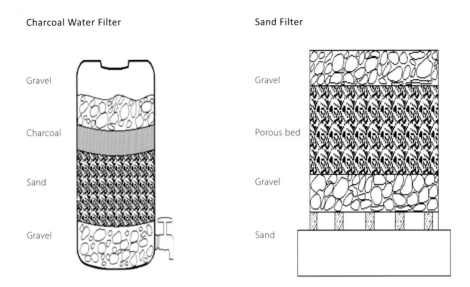

Charcoal Water Filter   Sand Filter

The common off-site treatment systems are:
• Activated sludge treatment
• Trickling filtration
• Constructed wetlands
• Simple anaerobic systems
• Upflow Anaerobic Sludge Blanket (UASB)
• Lagoons or ponds
• DEWATS (Decentralised WastewaterTreatment Systems)
There are several variations and improvements of these systems. There are also several land based treatments, which are more suitable for arid and semi-arid regions.

6.1.1 Off-site Treatment Systems

6.1.1.1 Activated Sludge Treatment
It consists of a primary treatment, which consists of mechanical screening to remove the suspended solids. This includes: removal of light weight, gross materials; removal of heavier, finer materials like sand; sedimentation in tank to remove finer solids. This is followed by the secondary treatment. Here aeration is provided by mechanical means to the primary treated wastewater in an aeration chamber. The chamber contains activated sludge. Aerobic bacteria attached to the sludge consume the organic matter in the waste water. The waste water resides in the chamber for a few hours. The sludge formed as a result of the action of the bacteria is carried over to a sedimentation tank, where the sludge settles down. The sludge is pumped back to the aeration chamber.

6.1.1.2 Trickling Filtration
It also has a primary treatment, where mechanical screening of solids is done. The secondary treatment is done by passing the waste water through the trickling or biological filter. The filter is a bed of solid media, such as stones or special plastics etc. Its purpose is to provide a surface for the aerobic bacteria to attach and to allow flow of air. The bacteria attached to the solid media consume the organic

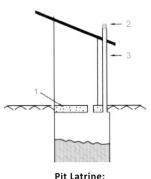

Pit Latrine:
1. Concrete plate
2. Flu screen
3. Vent pipe

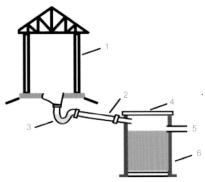

Pour and Flush La trine:
1. Superstructure
2. Connecting drain
3. Water-seal pan
4. Cover slab
5. Outflow
6. Lined

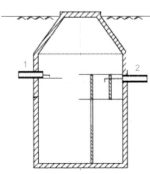

Septic Tank:
1. Inlet
2. Outlet

matter in the waste water. Aeration is by natural means, hence lesser energy is consumed. The sludge formed as a result of the action of the bacteria is carried over to a sedimentation tank, where the sludge settles down. The sludge is not pumped back. Compared to activated sludge process, the energy requirement is less, but the area required is higher. It can also be operated in batches, rather than continuously. (UNEPIETC, 2000)

6.1.1.3 Constructed Wetlands

Natural wetlands help protect water quality, by transforming many of the common pollutants in wastewater into harmless by-products or essential nutrients. This idea has led to the development of constructed wetlands that can be used for the treatment of pre-treated domestic or industrial waste water. Different wetland systems types and alternative plant species can be considered in constructed wetlands. It can be made on the surface like natural wetlands (Free Water Surface Systems) or the waste water can flow below the surface (Subsurface Flow Systems). It has a high treatment efficiency. The disadvantages are that of high cost, high space requirement, and that good care needs to be taken during the first 2 years. The Root Zone treatment system, is one such system developed in Germany. The land area required for a treatment plant is around 30-35 m²/m³ of waste water treated per day.

6.1.1.4 Upflow Anaerobic Sludge Blanket (UASB)

The UASB reactor contains a sludge blanket of anaerobic bacteria, which have developed into granules. Settled wastewater is passed upward through the reactor. The anaerobic action of the bacteria on the waste water produces carbondioxide and methane. The gases also helps in better mixing between the wastewater and the granules of bacteria. The granules are not carried over with the upflowing wastewater and hence a high concentration of bacteria is maintained in the tank. The treated effluent needs fur ther aerobic treatment to reduce its BOD and odour. (UNEP-IETC, 2000)

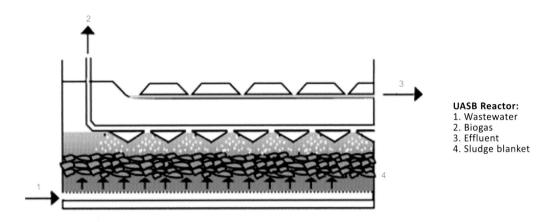

UASB Reactor:
1. Wastewater
2. Biogas
3. Effluent
4. Sludge blanket

6.1.1.5 Lagoons or Ponds

A lagoon is a shallow excavation in the ground (1 to 2m deep), into which the wastewater is collected. It is generally unlined and percolation of wastewater into the soil and groundwater takes place. They are effective in reducing BOD, and SS. Due to the longer residence time, in the order of days, pathogenic bacteria and viruses also die off compared to an activated sludge treatment plant. Most of the solids are removed by sedimentation. The aeration occurs naturally by diffusion and wind movement. The oxygen is supplemented by algae, which produces it photosynthetically in the presence of sunlight.

Three conditions could occur in the pond:
• Anaerobic: In this case anaerobic bacteria acts and methane gas is produced.
• Facultative: Whenever sunlight is present, algae produces oxygen and conditions are aerobic. Otherwise it is anaerobic. In such conditions, facultative bacteria acts, which can sur vive in both aerobic and anaerobic conditions.
• Aerobic: In this case aerobic bacter ia acts.
There could be a series of lagoons, the first one or two being anaerobic, the middle ones being facultative and the final ones aerobic. The sedimentation is mostly in the initial anaerobic ponds. They are simple to construct, have high pathogen removal rate, little maintenance, and high treatment efficiency. But they require large permanent space requirement.

6.1.1.6 DEWATS (Decentralised Wastewater Treatment Systems)

DEWATS is a concept that encourages the use of a combination of appropriate, lowcost, easy to operate and low maintenance sewage treatment technologies. It is based on the following treatment systems:
• Sedimentation and primary treatment in sedimentation ponds, septic tanks,or Imhoff tanks.
• Secondary anaerobic treatment in fixed bed filters or baffled septic tanks.
• Secondary and tertiary aerobic/anaerobic treatment in constructed wetlands or ponds. These systems are combined in accordance with the wastewater influent and

the required effluent quality.

6.2 Sludge Treatment

Sludge is mainly from 2 sources
• Sludge produced from waste water treatment. They consist of suspended solids and soluble solids conver ted to bacterial cells.
• Faecal Sludge

For safe use or disposal, they have to be stabilised aerobically or anaerobically, to reduce the BOD further. Two common methods are anaerobic digestion and composting. (UNEP-IETC, 2000)

6.2.1 Anaerobic Digestion or Bio-methanation

Bio-methanation is the process of conversion of organic matter in the waste (liquid or solid) to biogas and manure by microbial action in the absence of air (anaerobic digestion). The process has two benefits: it yields biogas, which can replace conventional fuels and it provides digested sludge, which can be used as a high nutrient fertiliser. The bacteria decompose the organic wastes to produces a mixture of methane and carbon dioxide gas (biogas). The process is maintained at around 35°C. After digestion, the sludge is passed to a sedimentation tank where it is thickened. The thickened sludge needs to be treated further prior to reuse or disposal. If needed, the gas can be used to heat the tank to maintain the temperature. (UNEP-IETC, 2000)

6.2.2 Composting

It is an aerobic process, where bacteria act on the sludge to produce more stable organic material (humus). The humus is very good as a soil conditioner. The optimum conditions are a moisture content of about 50 % and a carbon to nitrogen ratio of about 25 to 30 and a temperature of 55 °C . The carbon to nitrogen ratio is low (5 to 10) for wastewater sludge, since it is rich in nutrients. It is also high in moisture. Materials like dry saw dust, mulched garden wastes, forest wastes and shredded newspaper have a higher carbon to nitrogen ratio. They should be added to adjust both the moisture and carbon to nitrogen ratio. To destroy the pathogens, the temperature of 55 °C has to be maintained for 2 weeks. During this period, the material has to be turned every 2 to 3 days to ensure that the temperature is maintained throughout the compost and for proper aeration. This immature compost then should be allowed to mature for around 12 weeks, before it could be used. (UNEP-IETC, 2000)

6.3 Stormwater Treatment
Stormwater collects pollutants and solids along the path it moves. Separately collected stormwater can be treated by the following methods (UNEP-IETC, 2000)
• Filter strips: gently sloping vegetated area, where water is drained.
• Swales: long shallow channels, where water is drained.
• Filter drains and permeable surface: Water permeates through permeable surfaces and through permeable materials below the soil.
• Infiltration devices: Water is directed to soakways and infiltration trenches, located below the ground. Water is stored there and allowed to infiltrate into the soil.
• Basins and ponds: Storm water is directed into basins and ponds from where it infiltrates into the soil. Basins are storage area that is dry during dry weather. Ponds have water throughout the year.

7. Solid Waste Management
7.1 3R's - Reduce, Reuse and Recycling
The priority is in the order of reduce, reuse and recyle. Preventing or reducing the generation of waste is the best option. Wherever possible, the waste could be reused as it is. Recycling refers to the reprocessing of materials recovered from wastes, into a new product. This could also include processes such as composting and anaerobic digestion. It helps to reduce the use of virgin raw material and reduces energy use. Some materials like glass and metal can be recycled for any number of times. Other materials like paper can be recycled a few times only, due to the shortening of the fibres. Often, a certain amount of virgin material needs to be added for such

materials and this is termed as downcycling.

7.2 Anaerobic Digestion and Composting, explained in the section on sludge treatment, could be used for treating the organic solid waste.

7.3 Materials Recovery Facility (MRF)
The MRF is a facility that receives, separates and prepares recyclable materials from the waste, before sending them to potential users.

7.4 Mechanical Biological Treatment (MBT)
These are a flexible mix of mechanical and biological treatment methods, used to recover all type of resources from a mixed waste stream. The recovered materials could then be recycled. The mechanical part is similar to the MRF and the biological treatment normally consists of anaerobic digestion or composting. The process also may produce a fuel from the waste, termed as Refuse Derived Fuel (RDF).

7.5 Incineration
Incineration involves burning the wastes at high temperatures. It could be done with energy recovery or without energy recovery. In modern incinerators, hazardous and recyclable materials are removed, prior to combustion. It is considered useful for destroying pathogens and toxins at high temperatures, especially from clinical wastes. It is also attractive in countries having a shortage of land. A main concern in incineration is the emission of harmful pollutants like dioxin and furan.

7.6 Sanitary Landfills
Sanitary landfills are carefully designed landfills that prevent pollution of air, water and soil, and other risks to man and animals. Most of them have expensive and carefully constructed impermeable layers to contain leachates and drainage systems to take the leachate to a treatment plant or a storage tank. Aesthetic considerations are also taken into account.

Eco-housing Projects

Belvedere Residence

Location Belo Horizonte, Brazil
Architects Anastasia Arquitetos
Completion Date 2011
Construction Area 370m^2
Site Area 450m^2
Photos © Jomar Bragança

Good architecture is green. The way you position the building on the site, using the sunlight the right way, avoiding excessive heat gain and cross ventilation is enough in a privileged country (for climate reasons) like Brazil because it doesn't have extreme temperatures. Solar panels provide heating most part of the year. Massive concrete walls help to regulate the climate inside the house.

The architects avoided interfering in the original site, leaving it as natural as possible and designed a compact house, reducing its footprint in order to maximise the permeable area of the site. Indirect sunlight, pergolas and verandas protect the house from direct sunlight and provide the illumination they needed, so there is no need for artificial lighting during the day.

The 370-square-metre residence distributed in two levels is situated in a mainly residential neighbourhood in the city of Belo Horizonte, Brazil on a 450-square-metre flat site. The architectural approach seeks to privilege the maximum integration of external and internal areas, mixing up their boundaries, and then amplifying the feeling of wideness.

Due to the reduced size of the site, residual and crossing spaces were practically left out (for example, there is no entrance hall, in behalf of a visual permeability with the entrance garden, achieved through large pivotal doors in the façade).

The floor plan is rectangular and compact, stretching till the site's sidelines. The rooms are illuminated by large doors front and back façades and also by matted

glass locking (u-glass that acts as a good thermal insulation due to the existence of an air layer between the glass sheets) between the lagged cover labs. A glass cover over a concrete pergola complements the illumination through an indoor garden. Therefore, the house is flooded by zenithal and indirect natural light that besides avoiding artificial lighting during the day, also avoids excessive heat from direct sunlight. The prevailing wind comes from the street, thus the entering doors work as regulators of wind speed. Totally opened in the summer, praise cross ventilation, or closed in the winter, or even semi-opened if little ventilation is desired.

The residence was established in the street level, one metre above natural ground, in order to avoid unevenness and improve accessibility of the social areas. In addition, it also made the house more protected from the soil moisture. Solar collectors (that meet the needs of the house and the pool) occupy the most of the cover slab which prevented the use of this area initially contemplated.

Due to the large spans desired, supported by few points of foundation, and also to the large porch swing, the upper walls are concrete beams built by ripped forms of wood left apparent. Its aesthetics comes from a structural option, though it is not intended to be decorative.

The result was a light-weighted residence, lighted and ventilated, with pleasant and proportional spaces that puts into to practice the initial desire to the best possible use of external area.

1. Semi-open living room
2. Wall of the yard
3. Wood doors

Right:
1. Upper U-glass windows help to illuminate the house, avoiding the excessive heat of the north sun
2. Solar thermal roof panels are used to heat water
3. Concrete pergola, covered with glass, brings daylight to the house
4. Wood doors regulate the eastern wind, which crosses the house, taking off the heat

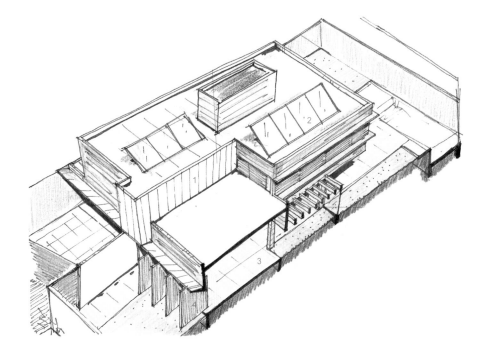

4. Living room /social space detail
5. Dining table
6. Living room interior

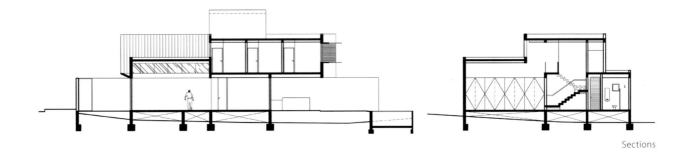

Sections

7. Private living room detail
8. Private living room and hallway

Ground Floor Plan:
1. Garden
2. Bedroom
3. Laundry
4. Living room
5. Dining room
6. Outdoor terrace
7. Swimming pool

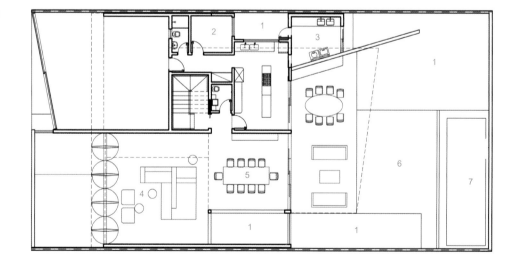

First Floor Plan:
1. Family room
2. Bedroom
3. Bathroom

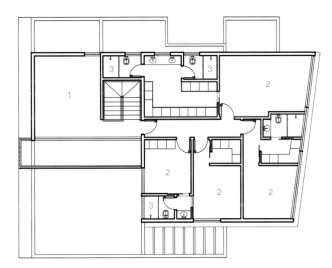

Carey House

Location Australia
Architects TT Architecture
Completion Date 2009
Total Surface Area 542 m^2
Photos © Red Zebra Photography
Award HIA Winner – Custom Built Home – Open Category, 2009

The Carey house client's brief reflects a 21st century reference to the confidence and optimism that lies at the heart of modernism stating that; "the house is to be a modern, contemporary residence of premium quality using materials not normally used in residential construction – steel, glass, metal cladding etc". In the client's own words "Understated but brave, edgy without being pretentious".

Responding to the brief involved exploring a core idea of one of the modern movement's most enduring legacies: the dissolution of the traditional boundaries between interior and exterior space. The design of the house explores the notion of a primary space being "one room thick". The voluminous central space promotes good cross ventilation and a high degree of hot air "purging" in summer. The design responds to give regionally and seasonally appropriate spaces. In physical form the referencing of Neutra is contained in the notion that the viewer's eye is drawn out by the long horizontal planes of the roof.

The design is not with just an exercise in planes and modernism; rather, it responds to the contemporary concern with resource sustainability. It makes strong gestures as a standalone, autonomous entity. The following initiatives are taken from concept to completion: "solar slot" orientation, high thermal mass, the inclusion of thermal chimney technologies.

The use of a hybrid semi-commercial "whole of building" heating solution includes the domestic hot water. The system consists of a solar evacuated

Elevations

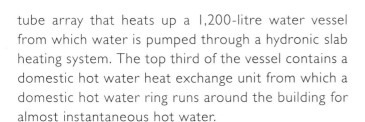

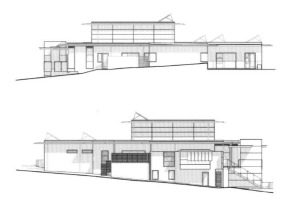

tube array that heats up a 1,200-litre water vessel from which water is pumped through a hydronic slab heating system. The top third of the vessel contains a domestic hot water heat exchange unit from which a domestic hot water ring runs around the building for almost instantaneous hot water.

There is a 5,000-litre capacity water harvesting system for use for the swimming pool, toilets and gardens. This has allowed an average daily use for a family of 4 of only 400 litres. There is also a 2,000 litre grey water re-cycling system and a 5KW "back to grid" photovoltaic array.

The use of high grade rock wool insulation provides superior levels of acoustic and thermal insulation including the careful infill around windows and doors to ensure the building was "air-tight".

In the resolution of the aesthetic and the technical, the house stands as a marriage of modern concerns to modernism gestures.

1. General view of façade
2. Exterior night view
3. Terrace night view
4. Balcony detail

Above:
1. Fascia to match Colourbond Surfmist
2. Cliplok or similar roof (amour grey)
3. Soffit gloss paint FC to match fascia
4. Vitrabond or similar aluminum composite metal panel – smoke silver
5. Anodised aluminum commercial windows (or similar)
6. Bush hammered concrete with stainless inset strips
7. Glass on batten pergola structure
8. Glass balustrades
9. Recycled timber cladding
10. Masonry walls white-painted render

5. Living room
6. Kitchen and bar

Main Floor Plan:
1. Bedroom
2. Rumpus
3. Games
4. Meals
5. Family
6. Kitchen
7. Dining
8. Lounge
9. Study
10. Walk-in wardrobe
11. Gym
12. Bathroom
13. Bathroom
14. Laundry

6

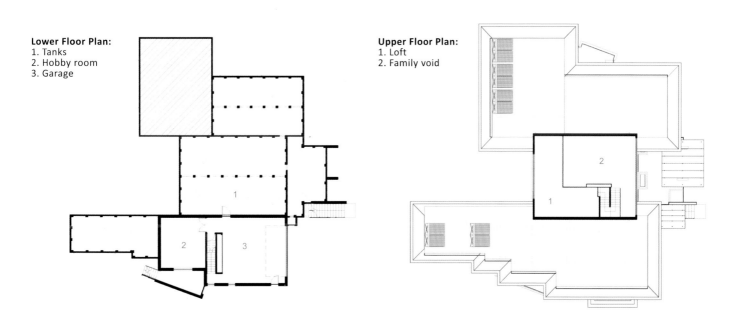

Lower Floor Plan:
1. Tanks
2. Hobby room
3. Garage

Upper Floor Plan:
1. Loft
2. Family void

700 Palms Residence

Location Venice, California, USA

Architects Steven Ehrlich Architects

Completion Date 2006

Total Surface Area 420m^2

Photos © Erhard Pfeiffer, Julius Shulman & Jeurgen Nogai, Grey Crawford

The exuberant Bohemian spirit of Venice, California, is expressed within urban residential constraints in the 700 Palms Residence.

The design maximises volume, light, and privacy on a narrow lot, with sensitivity to the scale of its eclectic neighbourhood of beach bungalows a half mile from the Pacific Ocean.

Raw, honest materials fit in with the grittiness of the Venice environment; the maintenance-free exterior of Corten steel, copper, and stucco weathers naturally, while interior surfaces are left unpainted.

The house dissolves the barriers between indoors and out, creating flexible spaces that take advantage of the benign climate. Built on an urban infill lot, the compound's orientation toward its lively neighbourhood is friendly while garden courtyards afford privacy.

Flexibility and transformation have been fully realised throughout the house. The wood-and-steel frame structure is outlined by a steel exoskeleton, from which electronically controlled light scrims roll down horizontally to shield the front façade from the western sun.

The juxtaposition of confined and monumental rooms animates the design; space is compressed at the low front entrance and then explodes into the main volume.

The 5-metre-high living-dining area opens up with sliding and pivoting glass doors on three sides; when opened entirely to the elements, the structure is an airy pavilion with temperate ocean breezes making air conditioning unnecessary. In winter, the iron oxide-infused concrete floors are radiantly heated.

The house design takes full advantage of the local climate such that a net zero energy building is obtained. This was done by employing a highly efficient building envelope and incorporating passive solar gains. Radiant floors and solar thermal energy are utilised for space heating and domestic hot water heating.

The house also relies on natural ventilation, thermal mass and operable shading to eliminate mechanical cooling, despite the large glazing areas. Finally, by employing ultra-efficient appliances and lighting and by incorporating solar electric power for the remaining loads, the house achieves its goal for a net zero energy home.

The chosen coating and maintenance-free exterior finish materials, including Corten steel and TREX (a sustainable material made of recycled plastic bags and sawdust), weather naturally, while all interior surfaces rely on varying tactile materials such as carnauba-waxed carbon steel and plaster which are left unpainted.

Three garden courtyards embrace three 60-year-old trees. The courtyards afford privacy and enhance the well-being of its occupants. The overall massing

1. Yard night view
2. Yard with palm

maximises volume and natural light gains on the narrow lot, yet displays sensitivity of scale to the eclectic neighbourhood of beach bungalows.

Exterior sunshades on an exoskeleton of steel control the heat gain from the southwestern exposure. Flexible, transformative spaces were created through the use of extensive operable glass doors.

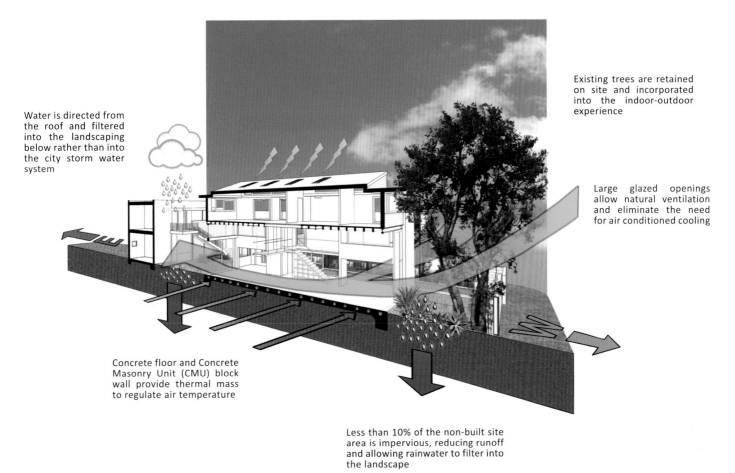

Water is directed from the roof and filtered into the landscaping below rather than into the city storm water system

Existing trees are retained on site and incorporated into the indoor-outdoor experience

Large glazed openings allow natural ventilation and eliminate the need for air conditioned cooling

Concrete floor and Concrete Masonry Unit (CMU) block wall provide thermal mass to regulate air temperature

Less than 10% of the non-built site area is impervious, reducing runoff and allowing rainwater to filter into the landscape

Left:

2. Horizontal and vertical retractable shades provide additional sun protection
3. Large glazed openings facilitate cross ventilation and negate the need for mechanical cooling
4. Concrete floor slab and exterior walls provide thermal mass to mitigate temperature differences
5. Drought-tolerant local plants used in a highly permeable planting bed
6. Outdoor decks and roof drains into filtering permeable planting beds below

3

3. Outdoor swimming pool
4. Loft bedroom with balcony

Elevation South

Elevation East

Elevation North

Elevation West

Section

5

5. Living room table
6. Living room

6

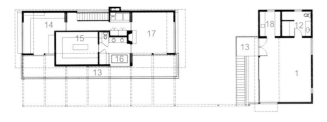

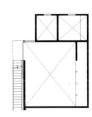

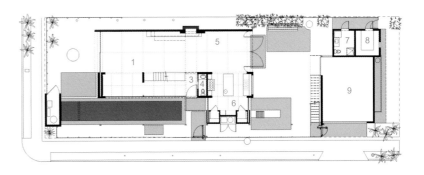

Floor Plans:

1. Living room
2. Pool
3. Entrance
4. Powder room
5. Dining room
6. Kitchen
7. Laundry
8. Storage
9. Garage
10. Bridge
11. Bedroom
12. Bathroom
13. Deck
14. Library
15. Closet
16. Master bathroom
17. Master bedroom
18. Kitchenette

7

7. Living room and stair to the upper floor
8. Stair detail
9. Bathroom

Private Residential House Leipzig Leutzsch

Location Leipzig, Germeny
Architects Andreas Thiele-Architekten
Completion Date 2010
Total Surface Area 145m^2
Photos © hiepler, brunier
Energy Consumption 59 kWh/m^{2}a

First of all, it has to be mentioned that the German laws and guidelines for new buildings define a very high standard regarding energy saving, use of renewable energy and use of building substances with a high balance of sustainable energy. The house in Leipzig naturally fulfills these regulations through its construction and its building services, and even exceeds these by making use of the technical facilities.

The construction is designed for minimum energy consumption – the technical building services are optimised for an efficient use of the primary energy, which is obtained from renewable energy (geothermal energy). The construction provides a thermal-inert mass that stores heat to a high degree and is insulated with a 20 cm layer of mineral insulation. The technical building services provide heating through a geothermal energy pump. Heating in the living- and bedrooms is provided by low-temperature panel heating on the walls, in the bathrooms and secondary rooms by low-temperature floor-heating.

In order to minimise loss of heating energy through ventilation, the house is equipped with a qualified heat-recovery ventilation system (incoming air in the living- and bedrooms, outgoing air in the bathrooms and secondary rooms). The ventilation system is supplied with heat exchangers that regulate the air humidity.

As far as it was sensible and possible in terms of construction, only materials complying with the

1

principle of sustainable energy were used. The shell construction consists mostly of mineral brickwork. The façade is rendered with a mineral insulation and mineral plaster. The wooden windows are triple glazed. The interior walls are rendered with mineral plaster. The floors are covered with wood and linoleum.

The site is located in the Leipzig district of Leutzsch, in an area mainly consisting of villas and one- and two-family residences, in close proximity to the Auenwald forest. The structure is rectangular and each floor steps back towards the garden. The living room and the study as well as the garden terrace are located on the ground floor. The upper floor includes the bedrooms, children's rooms and another terrace.

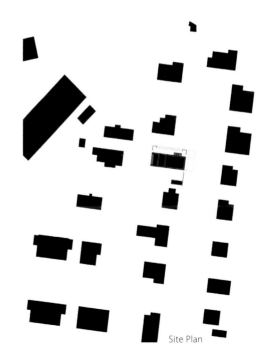

Site Plan

1. South-west elevation
2. North-east elevation
3. East elevation

Planning of Light

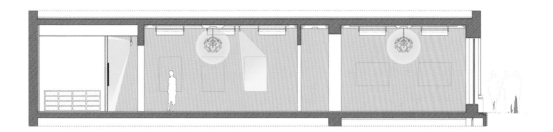

4,5. Dining room

Energy Concept Diagram:
1. Incoming air -
   wall heating
2. Outgoing air
3. Floor heating
4. Floor heating
5. Wall heating
6. Waste air
7. Fresh air
8. Heat exchange
   geothermal
   heat pump

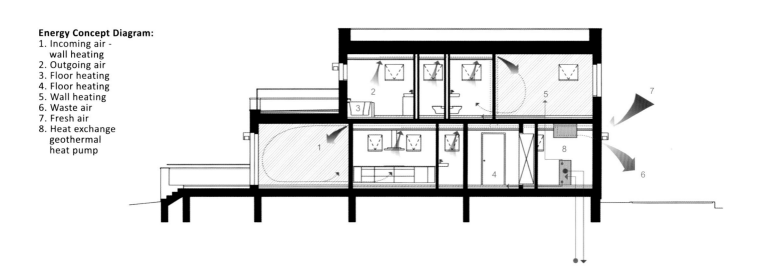

5

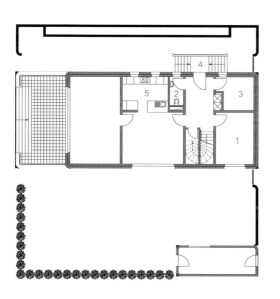

Floor Plan:
1. Ladder
2. WC
3. Storage
4. Entrance
5. Kitchen

6

6. Detail of the bathroom
7. Detail of staircase
8. Detail of the interior

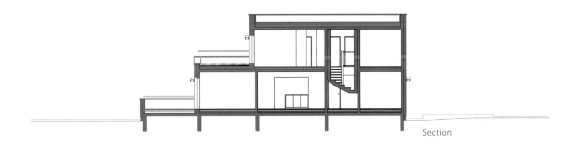

Section

Home for Life

Location Lystrup, Denmark

Architects AART architects A/S

Completion Date 2009

Construction Area 200m^2

Photos © Adam Mørk

Award 2010, The Green Good Design Award
initiated by The Chicago Athenaeum

Home for Life is designed as the world's first Active House – in other words it is designed to give more than take. The Active House vision defines highly ambitious long term goals for the future building stock. The purpose of the vision is to unite interested parties based on a balanced and holistic approach to building design and performance, and to facilitate cooperation.

Active Houses can be new-build or renovation. They can be homes, offices or public buildings. Active House proposes a target framework for how to design and renovate such buildings that contribute positively to human health and well-being by focusing on the indoor and outdoor environment and the use of renewable energy.

An Active House contributes positively to the energy balance of the building. It is energy efficient and all energy needed is supplied by renewable energy sources integrated in the building or from the nearby collective energy system and electricity grid.

Indoor climate creates a healthier and more comfortable life for the occupants. An Active House creates healthier and more comfortable indoor conditions for the occupants and the building ensures generous supply of daylight and fresh air. Materials used have a positive impact on comfort and indoor climate.

An Active House has a positive impact on the environment. It interacts positively with the

environment by means of an optimised relationship with the local context, focused use of resources, and on its overall environmental impact throughout its life cycle.

The 200m^2 single family house is designed as a CO_2-neutral demonstration project and thanks to 7m^2 solar collectors, 50m^2 solar cells and a solar heat pump the house is designed to produce more energy than it consumes. With an estimated energy surplus of 9kWh/m^2/year it takes approximately 40 years for the house to generate the same amount of energy that was used to produce its building materials.

The construction consists of a timber framing above a concrete raft, while the building is clad externally in slate fixed battens, and the floor tiles are mosaic made from recycled glass.

The window area (vertical windows and roof windows) is equivalent to 40 % of the floor area, making the daylight area of the house twice the size of the daylight area of a conventional low-energy building.

All roof windows are with triple glazing and fitted with interior decorative blinds and exterior awnings that protect effectively against heating in the summer (up to 90 %) and insulates against heat loss through the windows in the winter.

To ensure a healthy indoor climate, sensors register heat, humidity and CO_2 in all rooms and all roof

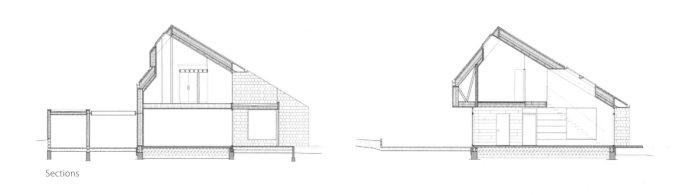

Sections

windows are with io-homecontrol®, which is an electronic control system that helps ensure a comfortable indoor climate and minimal energy consumption, e.g. by closing windows and blinds at night to avoid heat loss, thus minimising the energy loss at night considerably.

1. House and surroundings
2. Back façade
3. Façade-slate
4. Terrace
5. Front façade
6. General view of exterior

7,8. Dining room

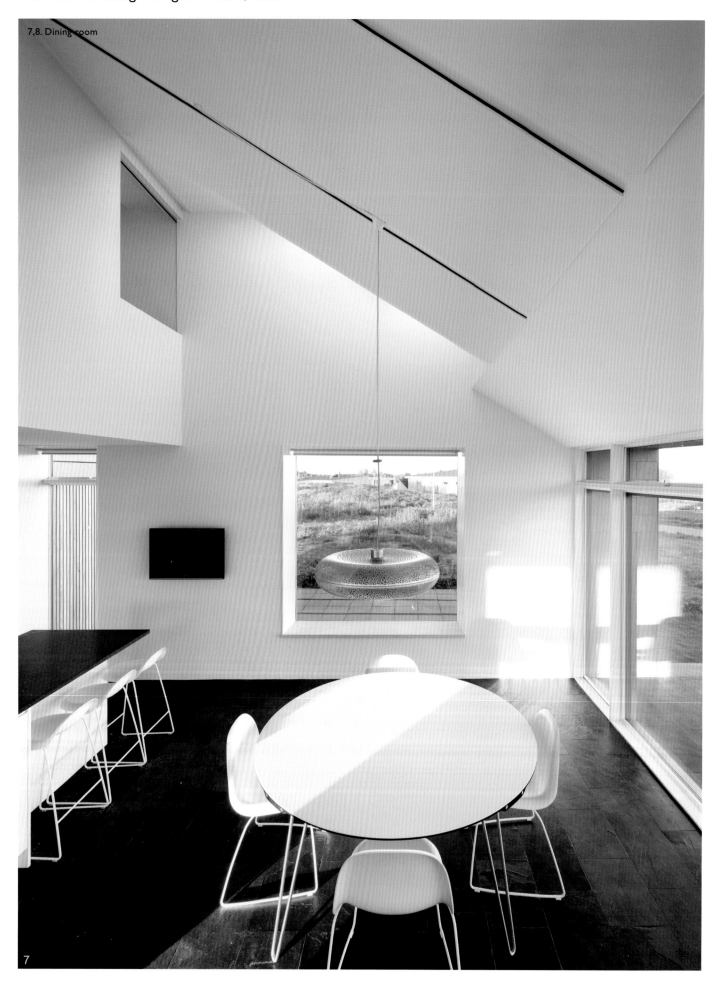

7. Dining room

Sustainable Design Diagram::
1. Energy-optimised windows exterior sun-screening
2. Thermal solar collectors (50 sqm – 5,500 kWh/year)
3. Solar cells (6.7 sqm – 2,100 kWh/year)
4. Electricity (installations household artificial light + energy)
5. Sunlight angel summer
6. Sunlight angel winter
7. Exterior sun-screening
8. Energy-optimised windows
9. Interior sun-screening / night insulation
10. Water tank
11. Info. display (sun-screening, natural ventilation, mechanical ventilation, heating, light)
12. Solar heat pump (4,200 kWh/year)
13. Floor heating system
14. Ventilation / heat recycling
15. Energy-optimised windows
16. Natural ventilation

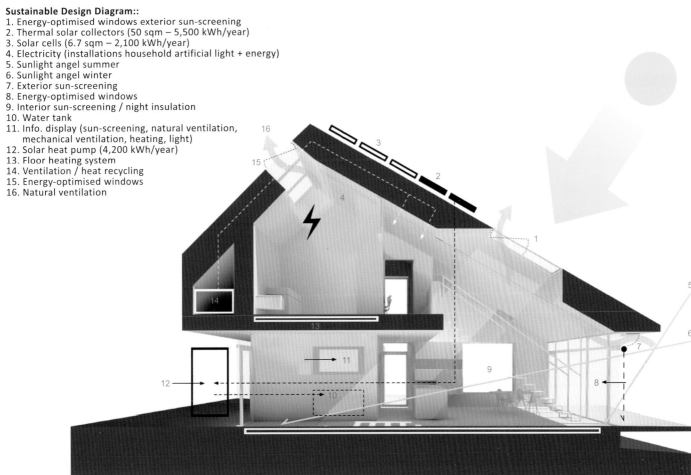

First floor plan (Left):
1. Bedroom
2. Terrace
3. Attic
4. Bathroom
5. Balcony
6. Master bedroom
7. Terrace

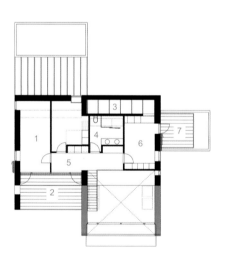

Ground floor plan (Above):
1. Annex
2. Garage
3. Pergola
4. Living room
5. Entrance
6. Bathroom
7. Technique
8. Scullery
9. Annex with pantry
10. Kitchen & dining
11. Roofed terrace
12. Terrace

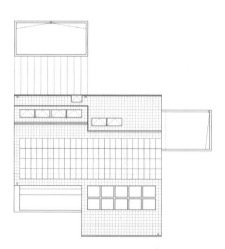

9,10. Stairs viewed from the dining room
11. Close up of interior

O-S House

Location Racine, USA
Architects Johnsen Schmaling Architects
Completion Date 2010
Energy Consumption 41.6 MMBtu/year
Photos © John J. Macaulay

The O-S House is a small infill residence in Racine, Wisconsin, a rustbelt city epitomising the painful urban decline of Middle America's manufacturing centres. Commissioned by a young family, the project is one of the first LEED Platinum homes in the Upper Midwest and demonstrates how a small, sustainable residence built with a moderate budget can become a confident, new urban constituent, a harbinger of change in a city suffering from decades of economic stagnation and urban disinvestment.

Situated on a vacant urban parcel, the project repairs the street edge and adds immediate density to a well-established neighbourhood in this old Midwestern city, avoiding the environmental calamities unavoidable in the development of suburban green fields or productive farmlands.

The local climate, with its very cold winters and hot, humid summers, required a careful mix of active and passive design strategies to ensure proper interior conditioning. The structure is elongated along the north-south axis to take advantage of the cool eastern lake breezes during the summer, and high-performance low-E, argon-filled operating windows in all rooms provide cross-ventilation throughout the house. A centrally located staircase functions as a thermal chimney, allowing warmer air on the main level to escape through operable windows in the upper observatory. The large southern overhang minimises solar heat gains in the summer while harnessing the sun's power in the winter. Likewise, the foliage of the old maple tree on Main Street serves as a natural umbrella for the house. The north façade, exposed to brutal northern winter winds,

was kept windowless to eliminate the possibility of air leakage.

The building volume is wrapped in an 8'' deep rain-screen system designed to reflect solar radiation and allow moisture to escape with the flow of air behind the suspended concrete façade panels. As a result, the underlying thermal envelope is protected from direct solar exposure and moisture, directly improving the relative comfort zone of the occupants inside.

Day-lighting and natural ventilation played paramount roles in the design of the house. Windows were precisely sized and located so that daylight penetrates deep into all parts of the house, virtually eliminating the need for artificial lighting throughout the day, even when it is cloudy. The main level, where the majority

of common activities take place, is generously glazed to enhance the visual connectivity between inside and outside, while the fenestration on the upper level, where the rooms are private, is more restrained.

The combination of operable windows and shallow building volume allows for a high degree of natural cross-ventilation. In the winter months, when natural cross-ventilation is impractical, the house is mechanically ventilated utilising a dedicated outdoor air supply system that, in conjunction with a heat recovery system, provides fresh air to the occupants. In addition, only low-VOC and VOC-free paints and cabinetry were used, minimising off-gassing and toxic air pollutants inside the house. The garage is mechanically exhausted and its walls and ceiling completely sealed to prevent contaminants from entering the house.

It was important to maintain a completely permeable site after construction to avoid further straining of the city's sewer system. The building's roof feeds about 65% of rainwater into a designated groundwater percolation area via rain chains and drainage tiles; the remaining rainwater is directed into two large rain barrels, where the water is stored and used for incidental maintenance projects and a small vegetable garden. All landscaping, selected and placed strategically to act as permanent erosion control, is native and drought tolerant, requiring essentially no irrigation after taking root.

Inside, the house features a compact structured plumbing system with low-flow fixtures throughout and an on-demand hot water circulating pump, significantly reducing water consumption. The family also decided to forgo a dishwasher and selected the most water-efficient Energy Star-rated washing machine available at the time.

Heating and cooling is provided by a geothermal ground-source heat pump with a vertical loop system. The envelope of the house is super-insulated with an agricultural based closed cell expanding foam insulation. Innovative wood framing techniques were deployed, including two-stud corners that avoid the fully-blocked "cold" corner detail typically used in residential construction, and wall studs at 24" on centre instead of 16", which decreases thermal bridging and increases the insulated surface area.

About 70% of the electric power consumed in the house, which is equipped with fluorescent and

1. Façade viewed from lawn
2. House in dusk
3. Side façade

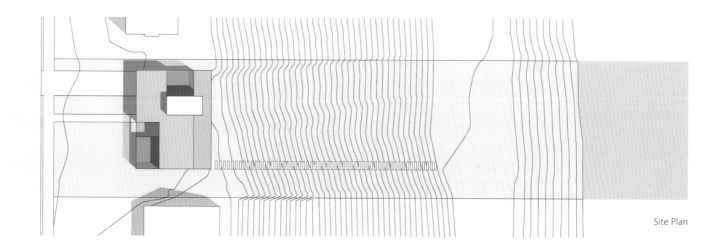

Site Plan

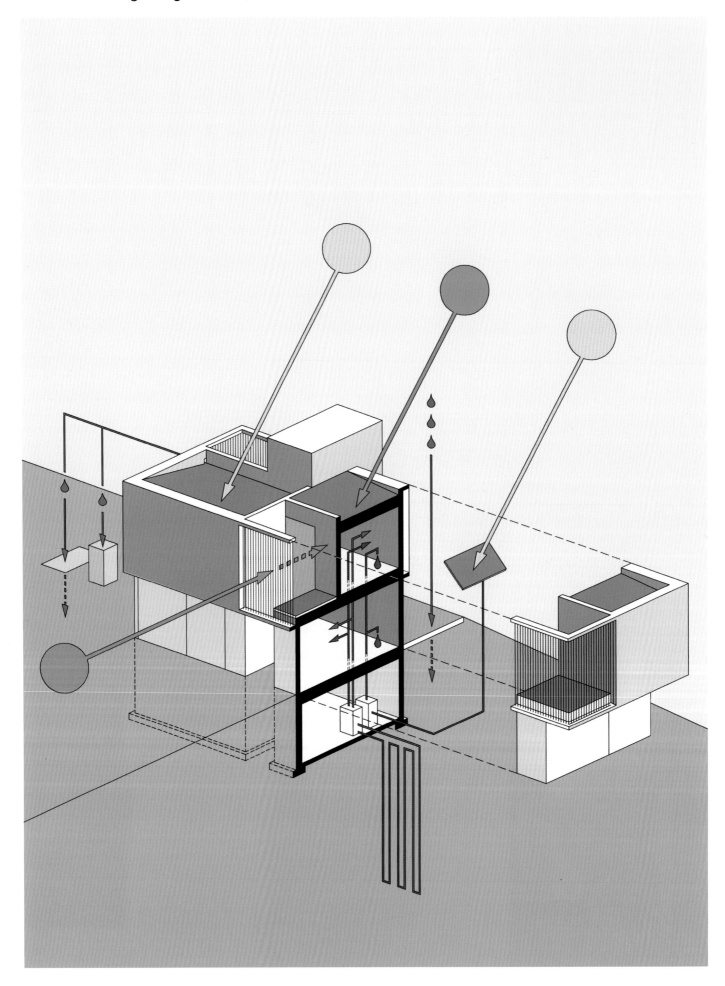

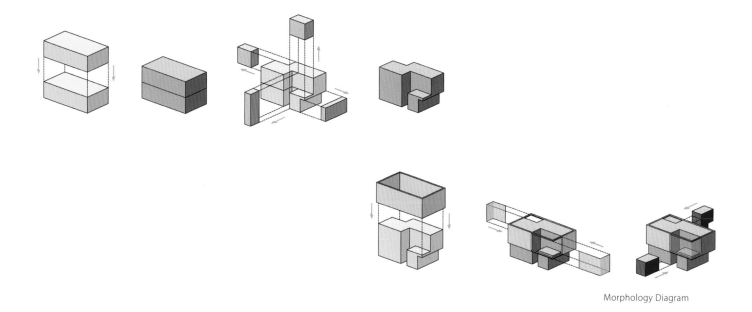

Morphology Diagram

LED fixtures throughout, is generated by a 4.2kw photovoltaic system, utilising PV laminates adhered to the roofing membranes as well as a free-standing array. In the summer, excess power from the PV system is purchased at a premium by the utility company and fed back into the grid. As technology advances and prices for photovoltaics decrease, additional arrays can be installed to eventually achieve complete energy independence.

Hot water is generated by a solar hot-water panel that preheats the water, backed up, as necessary, by a tankless hot-water heater. Insulated pipes and an on-demand pump efficiently distribute the hot water.

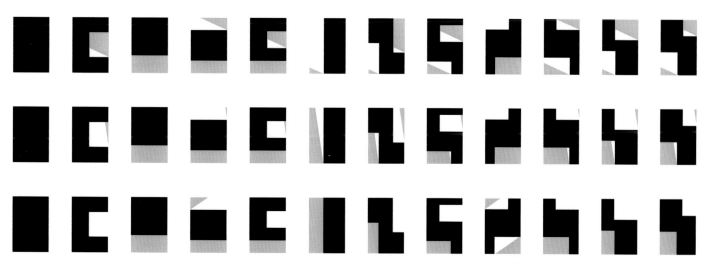

Solar diagrams of the house

4

4. Upper observation deck
5. Kitchen detail

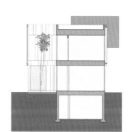

Sections

6. Mini study space
7. Bathroom detail
8. Wonderful waterside view
   through French window

Visual Permeability   Structural Walls   Rain-screen Wrapper   Outdoor Rooms   Solar Roofs   Storm Water Management

Floor Plan (Bottom):
1. Entry
2. Garage/bikes
3. Kitchen
4. Dining
5. Living
6. Entry courtyard
7. Bedroom
8. Bath
9. Observatory
10. Outdoor room
11. Solar roof
12. Permeable patio

  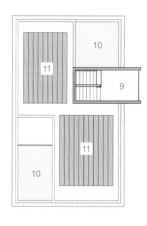

Higgins Lake House

Location Roscommon, USA
Architects Jeff Jordan Architects LLC
Completion Date 2011
Construction Area 446m^2
Photos © Jeff Garland Photography

Many families in Michigan share a tradition of spending weekends and vacations in cottages adjacent to the state's collection of lakes.

Higgins Lake is considered one of the most spectacular of the inland lakes and the empty-nester's who commissioned this cottage wanted to be able to share this resource with their large family and many friends. In order to do so, they requested a large gathering area for cooking, eating and relaxing and space to sleep twenty adults.

Given the relatively large size of the cottage compared to the neighbouring houses, the central challenge of this project is fitting a large building onto a narrow site without overwhelming the neighbours, but still taking advantage of the views.

The architects' solution locates the house in the centre of the site and breaks the overall volume of the building down into four smaller volumes to better incorporate it into the surroundings. Additionally, this strategy brings substantial amounts of light and air into every room of the house while allowing for views out to the lake and surrounding forest.

The living quarters and master suite are located above grade while the remaining bedrooms are partially buried to further diminish the apparent size of the house. The living quarters have a large expanse of glass facing the lake and additional glazing along the south side of the house to take advantage of passive heating in the winter. A large deck on the lake side of the house provides views while extending living space in the warmer months.

1

The Higgins Lake House draws from current sustainable thinking without trying to be a symbol of that movement. The architects positioned living spaces along the south side of the house with large expanses of glass to take advantage of passive winter heating, while providing deep overhangs to block summer sun. They minimised north-facing windows to reduce winter heat loss. Operable clerestory windows and skylights allow for summer cooling by simple cross ventilation.

All exterior walls and roofs cavities are filled with a closed cell spray foam insulation that virtually eliminates air infiltration. When coupled with a heat recovery unit, fresh air can be provided that is pre-conditioned to indoor temperatures resulting in heating and cooling costs way below average for a

house of this size. Low flow plumbing fixtures and dual flush toilets are used throughout.

Materials are locally sourced to the extent possible. A wood rain-screen siding system minimises heat gain from exterior surfaces by reducing the ability for heat to conduct through the wall assembly. In short, the project employs multiple sustainable strategies effortlessly and to great effect.

The Higgins Lake House uses materials that are locally sourced including oak hardwood flooring, framing lumber and wood siding. Spray foam insulation is composed of plant material. Metal roofing is recycled and will have long life reducing material costs and consumption in the future.

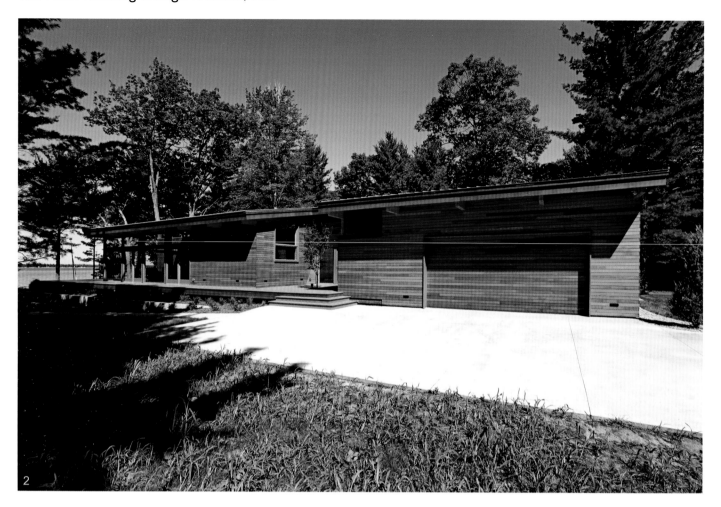

1. Terrace
2. House and surroundings
3. Side view

The Higgins Lake House is positioned in a way that best takes advantage of its surroundings. Views of the lake are provided while extensive landscaping nestles the house into its surroundings. Water for the small lawn is pumped from the lake and allowed to drain back without any chemicals or fertiliser added.

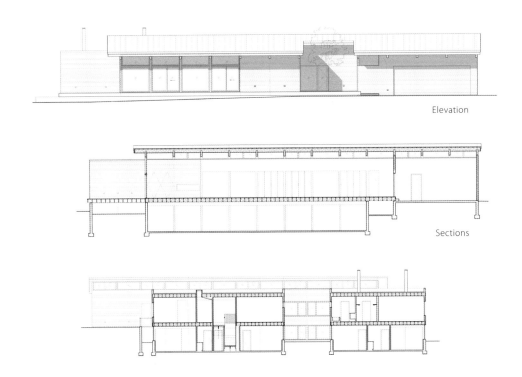

Elevation

Sections

4

5

4. Waterside view from the terrace
5-7. Detail of façade material

6

7

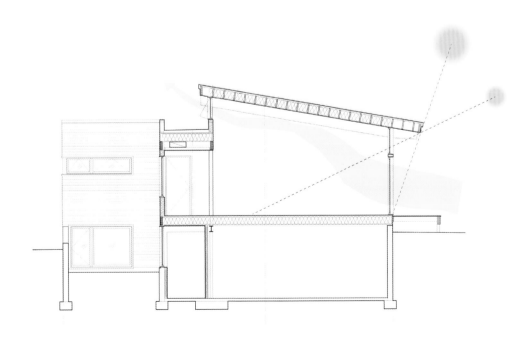

8. Living room
9. Kitchen and dining table

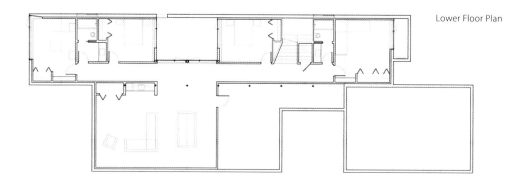

Lower Floor Plan

Upper Floor Plan:
1. Kitchen
2. Living
3. Dining
4. Master bedroom
5. Master bathroom
6. Master closet
7. Entry
8. Laundry
9. Bathroom
10. Bedroom
11. Study
12. Garage
13. Porch
14. Storage
15. Courtyard

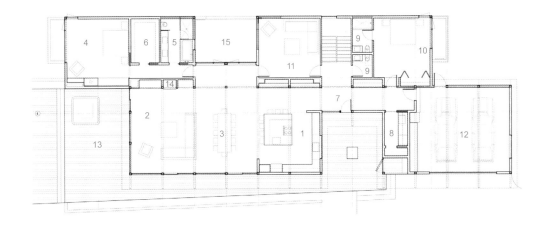

House V

Location Munich, Germany
Architects Architekturbüro Jakob Bader
Completion Date 2010
Area 210m^2
Energy Consumption 16.9kWh/m^{2}a
Photos © Kai Arndt

House V is a large house on a small plot of land and an even smaller budget. On the outside it is very red and on the inside very raw.

The house is well insulated and includes a geothermal pump and air-handling system minimising operation and maintenance costs. House V is not specifically an "Environmental" house but rather just simple and smart.

Arrival at House V is from the south. Cars are not hidden away in a garage but displayed under the house's wide upper storey cantilever which provides ample protection from the elements. This cantilever houses a large study and underneath it the main entry to the house and also a separate entry which is a shortcut to the loft space.

House V's outer T-form is mirrored on the inside: the central services zone is bordered on two sides by the larger living rooms. The central zone includes stairs, two bathrooms and two dressing rooms, a library and an internal chute linking the upper storey to the cellar. In the cellar there is plenty of storage space and the all-important control room, the holy crypt of the contemporary house where the technological controls for the house are located. The adjustment for these controls is by touch-screen, internet and iPhone for making changes when out and about.

Building House V was a specific challenge in itself. The strict council rules couldn't be compromised: e.g. the great upper storey is officially called just a pitched roof space. The setbacks from the boundary were also dealt with very artfully.

1

House V is modern but not perfectionist. It is outwardly sculptural and symbolic and inside raw and even abrasive; unlike many other contemporary houses which are smooth, sexy and dead boring. House V is human. The casual details are not spectacular but the concept: as a whole it is a harmony of volume, layout, façades, structure, technical configuration and inner organisation.

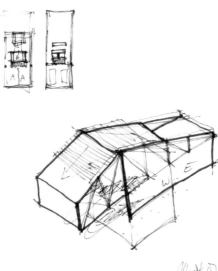

1. Façade
2. Living room night view from the yard

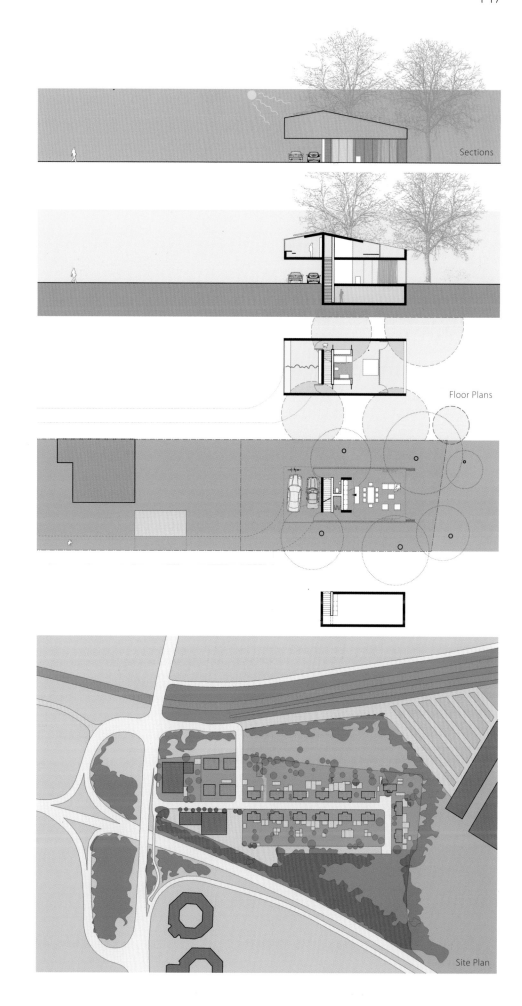

Sections

Floor Plans

Site Plan

3. Dining room
4. Dining table
5. Book shelves play the role of wall

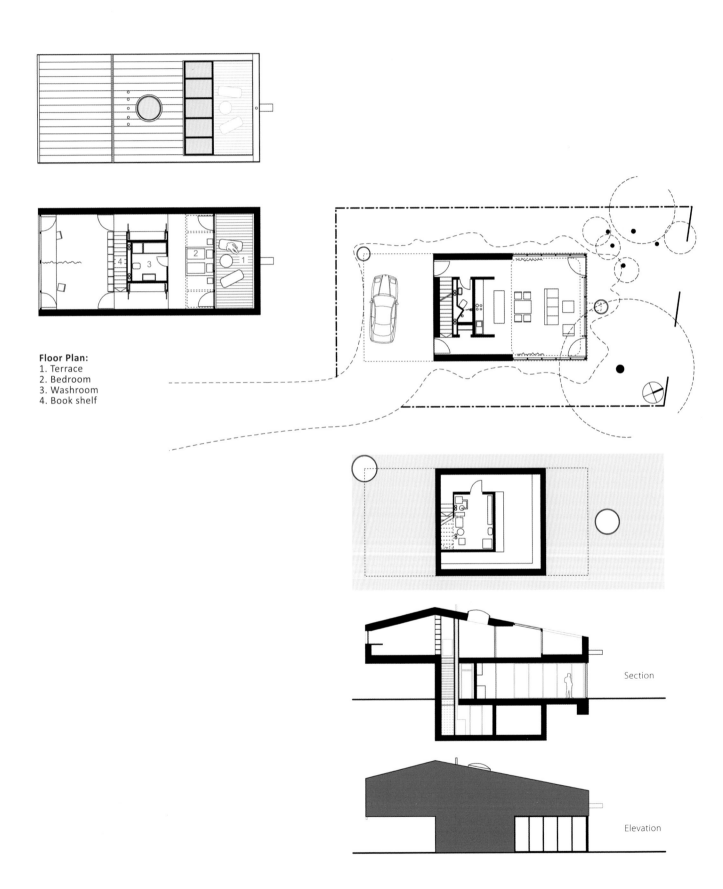

Floor Plan:
1. Terrace
2. Bedroom
3. Washroom
4. Book shelf

Section

Elevation

6. Bedroom with glass roof and wall
7. Bathroom

Chiaroscuro House

Location Carballo, Spain
Architects Mas Arquitectura
Completion Date 2009
Construction Area 370m^2
Photos © Ana Samaniego

The large windows distribution fills the house with natural light. Natural light is the distinctive sign of this house built on A Coruña (Spain). The design includes large windows in order to make the most of the brightness of this area.

On a plot only 9 metres wide, a three-storey house is built with large windows that spread natural light all around the rooms. The commitment to create a bright interior design is reflected in a skylight which cross the house perpendicularly, from the top floor to the living room, found on the ground floor, developing a geometric play of light and shades.

Inside, the sequence of open spaces avoids corridors, maximising the flow of movement around the rooms, all built with terraces. Having only one flight of stairs,

improves the movement between each floor.

The "Chiaroscuro" designed by architect Marcos Samaniego, from Mas Arquitectura, is reflected in the stark contrast between the pure white walls and the black colour we can find on the floor, curtains and carpentry. The house's bright atmosphere is an oasis for its tenants.

The architects try to place rooms, living rooms and other common spaces in south façade in order to take advantage of sunlight entrance. "Chiaroscuro House", as it is called this project, was built on a narrow plot of 9 metres wide. They opt to use only 6 metres and "stretch" the design to keep free south façade. Inside, layout includes opening fronts in three façades in order to achieve a suitable air circulation.

The house was built using traditional materials. Indeed the architects opt for using a special cement that allows them to increase house's thermal lag.

In this project the main tool to make the house sustainable is natural light. The architects believe that sunlight has got enough calorific power to cut down heating consume in a temperate climate as they have in Spain. For this reason, the architects design a wide skylight which distributes natural light to all rooms. As a result, the architects are able to keep a nice temperature inside in the winter as well as in the summer.

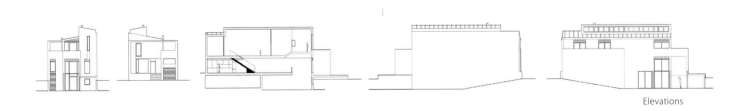

Elevations

1. Side view of the house
2. Back of the house
3. Structure in detail
4. Terrace

Sustainable Design Diagram:
1. Sunlight
2. House
3. South-facing frontage to increase sunlight and heat in the winter
4. Narrow plot of 9 metres between diving walls – House is built
   using only 6 metres to keep free south frontage
   in order to increase sunlight capture
5. Sunlight, chimney effect
6. A wide skylight goes through the house to
   keep natural light in common rooms and bathroom
7. Sunlight
8. Hot air
9. Fresh air
10. Elements for a great thermal lag: Solar support, Microcement
11. Interior air circulation three of four opening
    fronts for an air circulation
12. Fresh air
13. Emission of accumulated heat
14. Hot air
15. Ventilation
16. Hot air

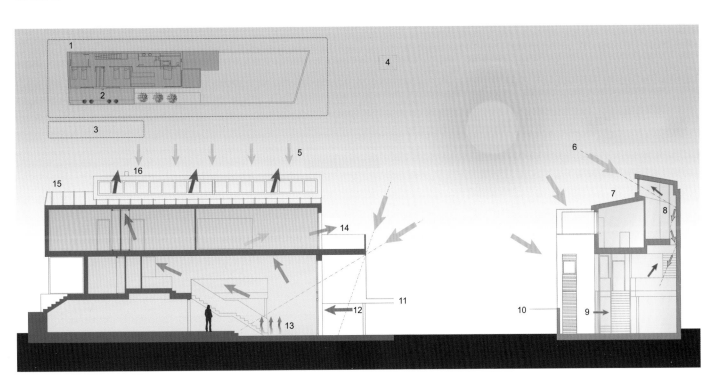

5

5. Living room viewed from the staircase
6. Stairs detail
7. Ceiling

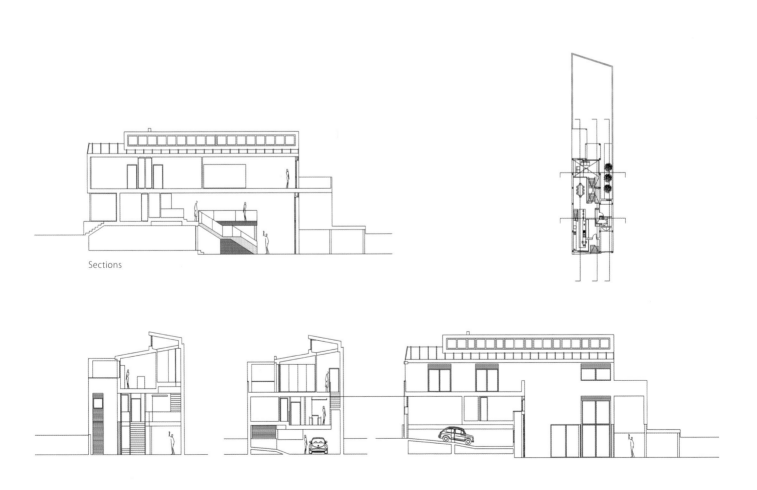

Sections

8. Staircase
9. Kitchen
10. Interior detail

11. Corridor
12. Bathroom
13. Walk-in changing room
14. Bedroom

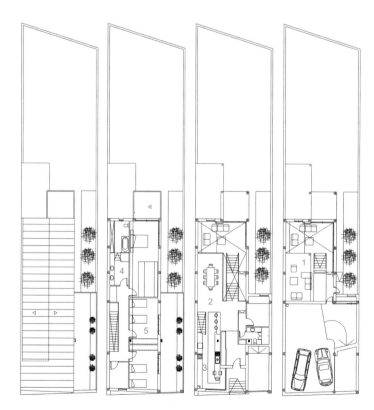

Floor Plan:
1. Living room
2. Dining room
3. Kitchen
4. Bathroom
5. Bedroom

13

14

Gandario

Location A Coruña, Spain
Architects Mas Arquitectura
Completion Date 2009
Construction Area 223m^2
Photos © Ana Samaniego

The warmth of the traditional designs perpetuates on light forms in this house placed on A Coruña (Spain).

Quality materials and warm spaces have been characterising the Galician traditional architecture since the XV century. Marcos Samaniego architect, from Mas Arquitectura, a young Spanish study, has added a new element to this tradition: the design. As a result, this house has been built in A Coruña. The architect has added enamel wood to Galician traditional material, stone, in order to maintain the warmth of the house.

However, the bioclimatic plan of the house leads to a simple-line design, with large windows in the walls in order to allow nature comes into the interior space. The carpentries, which are introduced into the stone walls, make stronger the structure.

The interior is emphasised by brightness and warm colours. In addition, the sun light gets over all the spaces from a skylight on the main floor. In the kitchen, you can find smooth surfaces and design furniture.

Details are very important in this house. The main staircase, covered by oak wood, receives the light from the large window and it is decomposed creating a hand-made library.

To sum up, this house means a small transformation of the Galician traditional architecture, an avant-garde wink in a traditional house.

Incorporate bioclimatic criterion is nowadays an indispensable requirement for house designers. It's essential to take into account different aspects like layout,

materials and energetic technology in order to build a sustaintable house. In Mas Arquitectura the architects share this theoretical positioning and bet for taking it to practice. This project, Gandario, is characterised for its south orientation to take advantage of natural light. Interior layout was developed to keep a pleasant temperature all year. Ventilation and insulation systems contribute to it. As a result, heating and air-conditioned use is minimum. The architects opt to build this house using local stone. Stone's bioclimatic advantages are

well-know. The resistance, no need maintenance and high thermal lag turn stone into a suitbale material for green house. The architects complete the build with wood, another bioclimatic material. This project includes a photovoltaic panel to supply electric energy to the house. It was placed in south façade in order to increase its performance. Also, the house has got a cassete fireflace with moveable grids in every room. This system, feed by wood, allows us to achieve a heat harmonic distribution.

Elevations

1,2. General view of exterior
3. Side view of house
4. Canopy

Sustainable Design Diagram:
1. Ventilation and insulation systems contribute to keep a pleasant temperature all the year
2. Cassete fireplace: high calorific power. Moveable grids in every room to a heat harmonic distribution
3. Hot air
4. Sunlight
5. Photovoltaic panel: it supplies energy to the house cutting electricity charge
6. Sunlight 70° summer
7. Sunlight 30° winter
8. South face: porch to regulate sunlight effect in summer-winter
9. Fresh air
10. Caviti: A right ventilation avoids ground's dampness from affecting the building. Also, it prevents gas accumulation
11. Emission of accumulated heat
12. Ventilation
13. Elements for a great thermal lag: interior face built using drilling brick and 6 cm insulation; Floor covered with heavy materials; 8 cm roof insulation

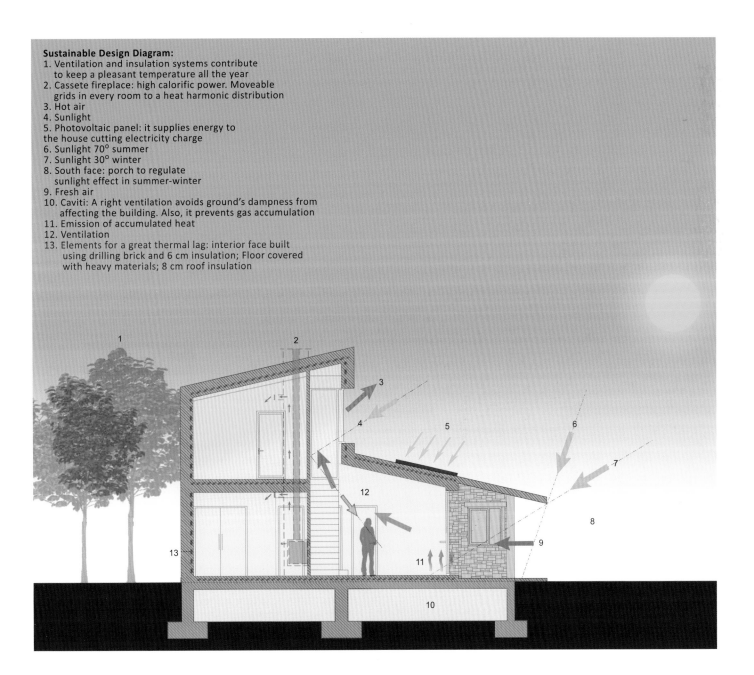

5. Dining room
6. Interior detail

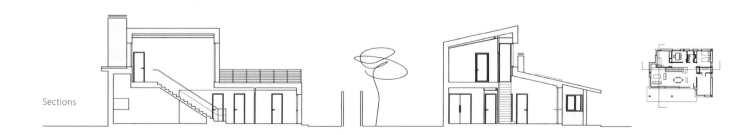

Sections

Floor Plan:
1. Dining room
   and living room
2. Kitchen
3. Study
4. Bedroom
5. Balcony
6. Bathroom

7. Bathroom
8,9. Kitchen

The Hillside House

Location Mill Valley, USA
Architects SB Architects
Completion Date 2010
Construction Area 196m^2
Photos © Mariko Reed,
Matthew Millman and Robert Bengston

Nestled in the hills of Mill Valley, California, just across the Golden Gate Bridge from San Francisco, this spectacular custom home has received certification as the first LEED for Homes Platinum custom home in Marin County, and one of only a handful in Northern California.

Carefully carved into steep hillside, and set amid towering oaks, this house is first and foremost a response to the site. "An authentic response deeply rooted in the site is absolutely the first step in sustainable design for any type of project," says Lee. The four-storey home steps back into the hillside, working its way around the trees, driven by the views, and defined by the intimate relationship between indoors and out. Private and living zones are set on their own floors, every space has its own private terrace, and every window embraces views of the surrounding trees or the San Francisco skyline in the distance. A covered terrace acts as an indoor/outdoor family room off the main living level, visually and psychologically expanding the space.

Built on an infill lot close to town, the house is designed to maximise solar orientation for the photovoltaic panels, as well as passive heating and cooling. The surrounding hillside provides the lower floors with natural insulation, solar power supplies electricity and hot water, and radiant floor heating and an innovative air re-circulation system condition the interior. A whole-house automation and lighting system, LED lighting, Fleetwood super-insulated doors and windows and indigenous, drought-tolerant landscaping conserve resources.

Local availability, recycled content and sustainable production drove the selection of each material, appliance and detail – including Western Red Cedar siding, Energy Star-Rated Whirlpool appliances, Kohler low-flow plumbing fixtures, Mythic zero-VOC paints, high-recycled content interior concrete from Concreteworks, sustainably produced stone veneers from Eldorado Stone, sustainably harvested floors and cabinetry from Plantation Hardwoods and New World Millworks, reclaimed timber and recycled metal roofing. Design elements crafted locally from reclaimed materials – such as hand-crafted tile from Sausalito-based Heath Ceramics and steelwork from artisan Brian Kennedy – give this project deep roots in the community, making it sustainable from a community standpoint.

Every inch of this LEED Platinum custom home has been designed to maximise its sustainability, in direct response to the site, trees and views. Consequently, this home lives far larger than its actual footprint, but with an impact that is far less.

The design of this home incorporates recycled and repurposed materials throughout including:
• Roof framing and exposed ceilings are made of reclaimed Douglas Fir, from a deconstructed seed plant.
• Concrete countertops from throughout the project are made with 74% post-consumer recycled glass, 15% post-consumer fly-ash.
• Windows contain 40-50% post-consumer recycled aluminum.
• Laundry countertops are made entirely from

recycled magazines.
• Interior stairwell walls are clad in re-purposed scaffolding beams, rendered unsuitable for their original use due to changes in OSHA standards.
• Exterior pendants are constructed from re-purposed steel buoys, rescued from Puget Sound.
• Simulated stone on exteriors is made with high recycled content.

This project has been designed to maximise opportunities for passive solar and insulation on this site. Nearly 20% of the home's square footage lies below grade, tucked into the steep hillside site and taking advantage of the opportunity for natural insulation. Extensive operable fenestration in every room takes full advantage of passive solar gain and natural ventilation, while automatically programmed shading prevents heat loss.

This project utilises the following systems to maximise energy efficiency:
• Home automation system: home automation system controls audio/visual, shading, air intake/exhaust fans, security and lighting. The system is programmable, and contains automatic controls to maximise efficiency.
• Solar Power, (3.75 kilowatt solar panels)
• Radiant heating: pre-heated by solar panels, and captures excess heat from the high-efficiency water heater.
• Thermal insulation: enhanced with a spray-in, soy-based foam insulation
• High-efficiency windows
• Automatic shading system
• Energy Star appliances
• LED Lighting

1. General view of exterior
2. House and surroundings

3. Exterior view
4. Exterior view of house and deck
5. View toward bedrooms from rooftop lawn(yoga deck at left)
6. Deck and lawn

Representative Green Features (Below):
1. Exterior cladding - Sustainable Western Red Cedar
2. Wood flooring - Engineered Plywood
   with Black Walnut Veneer
3. Roof framing / Exposed Ceiling - Reclaimed Lumber
4. Trellises and Exposed Week Posts - Reclaimed Lumber
5. Cabinetry - Forest Stewardship
   Certified Plywood Product
6. Interior Wall Surface (Stair Core)
- Reclaimed Scaffolding Boards
7. High Efficiency Drip Irrigation System
8. Synthetic Turf
9. Efficient Fixtures & Energy Star Appliances
10. Thermal Insulation
11. High Efficiency Windows -
    Made with Recycled Aluminum
12. Automated Shading System
13. LED Lighting
14. Concrete Countertops (Recycled Materials)
15. Simulated Stone Exterior Surfaces -
    Made From Recycled Materials

A. Rain water recirculation
B. Solar energy panels
C. Solar hot water
D. Passive solar
E. Operable fenestration,
   allows natural ventilation
F. Living room
G. Dining
H. Kitchen
I. Bedroom (guest)
J. Yoga deck
K. Entry porch
L. Master terrace
M. Master room
N. Master closet
O. Garage
P. Bedroom 2
Q. Elevated
R. Water recirculation
S. Radiant heat

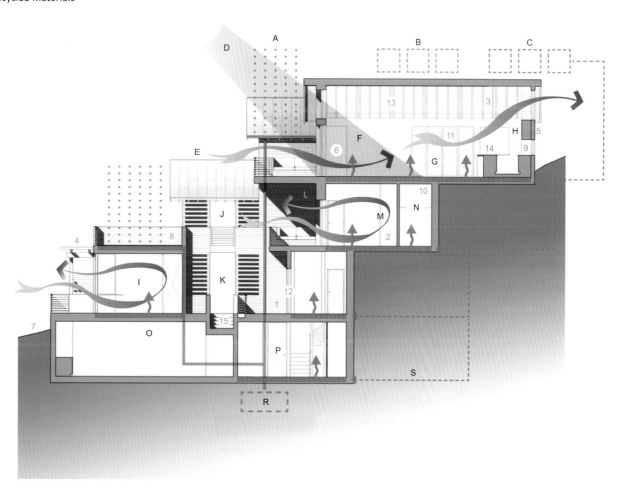

7. Corridor
8. View of the living, dining room, deck and hills
9. Pattern on the dining-room table
10. Dining room

11

11. View of indoor, outdoor room & living room beyond
12. Dining room and kitchen

13

13-15. Staircase and aisle
16. Bedroom
17. Outdoor bath
18. Master bedroom
19. Master bathroom

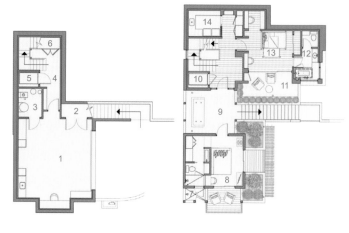

Floor Plan (Above):

1. Garage	9. Entry porch	17. Elevator	25. Dining
2. Trash	10. Elevator	18. Master terrace	26. Kitchen
3. Utility	11. Terrace	19. Master bath	27. Outdoor kitchen
4. Mud	12. Bath 2	20. Master bedroom	28. Fire pit
5. Elevator	13. Bedroom 2	21. Dressing	29. Outdoor family
6. Wine	14. Laundry	22. Baby	30. Powder room
7. Outdoor shower	15. Lawn	23. Upper terrace	31. Office
8. Bedroom (guest)	16. Yoga deck	24. Living	32. Elevator

16

17

18

19

BC House

Location Monterrey, Mexico
Architects GLR arquitectos – Gilberto L. Rodríguez
Completion Date 2010
Construction Area 1,200m²
Photos © Jorge Taboada

The project is in a privileged topographic situation, due to its visual condition of greater height in relation to the surrounding neighbours. This allows the house to enjoy excellent vistas towards the National Park of Chipinque in the south, as well as towards all of the east, which is dominated in the horizon by the "Cerro de la Silla", an emblematic hill in the boundaries of the city of Monterrey.

The proposed access to the site is located in the north side of it, ascending through a long slope that leads you to the highest level, where the floor plan is located.

With simple, pure geometric volumes, but rather challenging structural solutions, the project intends to evoke an image of lightness within a language of heavy and massive volumes. Although colour does not have yet an important presence in the work, this project takes an important step forward into the exploration of new materials, as it is the black granite and the white exposed concrete, in addition to the personality that the great amount of exposed steel elements gives to the building.

Finally, it is important to mention that beyond its bio-climatic function, the implementation of green roofs as a way to integrate the landscape, trying to conserve the natural surroundings of the zone, always dominated by the presence of the splendid Sierra Madre mountain range.

The house was conceived as a "Sustainable House" since the beginning, so it has a study on energetic efficiency, which analyses the sun trajectory and the prevailing winds in diverse seasons of the year.

As a result of these studies, the house has diverse systems of isolation, like its double walls with poliisocianurate, an ecological insulator; double windows with low emissivity (Low-E) glass; systems of pluvial water harvesting and grey water treatment for irrigation, solar paddles for pool heating and garden illumination, solar water heaters, hydronic heating systems to reduce the power consumption, south oriented skylights, as well as a landscape project with native vegetation.

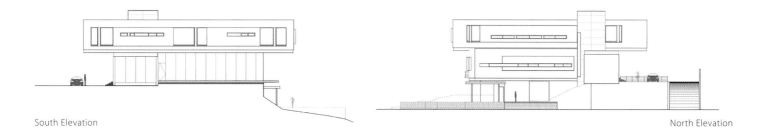

South Elevation

North Elevation

2

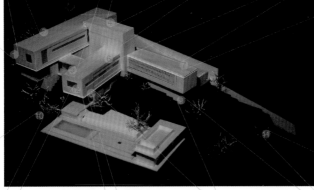

Sustainable System of the House:
1. Double wall thermal block and poliisocianurate insulation
2. Green roofs
3. Skylight facing south
4. Skylight facing south
5. Green roofs
6. Solar water heaters
7. Solar pool heating panels
8. Hydronic heating
9. Pluvial and grey water systems
10. Grey water treatment plant for irrigation
11. Xersicape garden
12. Double glazed windows with low-E glass

3

1. Side view of the house
2. General view of the house
3. Close view of the house

4

5

4,5. Swimming pool in the yard
6. View from garage

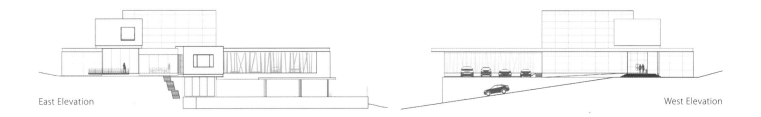

East Elevation

West Elevation

7. Parking lot
8. Corridor
9. Staircase

8 9

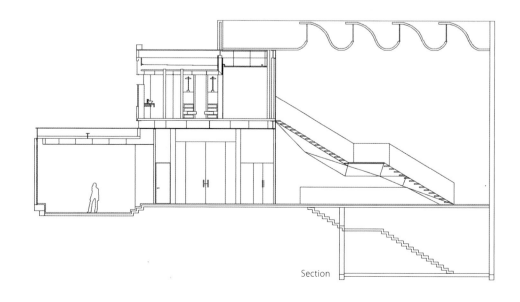

Section

10. Interior detail
11. Living room/social space
12. Dining room
13. Living room

12

13

Basement Plan:
1. Foyer
2. Covered terrace
3. Game room
4. Garage
5. Pool

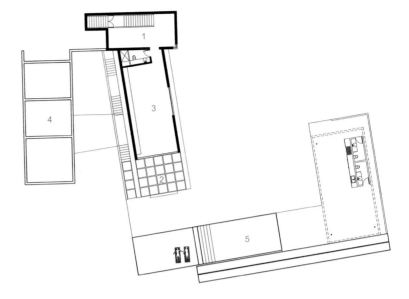

Level 1 Plan:
1. Foyer
2. Library
3. Living room 1
4. Living room 2
5. Dining room
6. Room connected to dining room
7. Service room
8. Laundry room
9. Kitchen

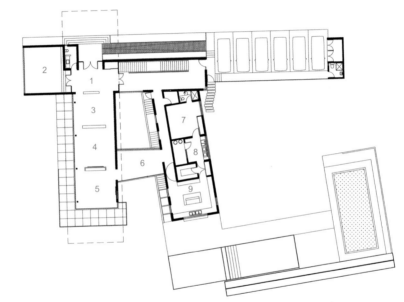

Level 2 Plan:
1. Foyer
2. Bedroom 1
3. Bedroom 2
4. Master bedroom
5. Dressing room master bedroom
6. Inside patio
7. Machine room

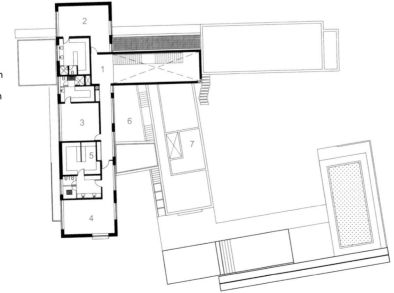

15

14. Living room/social space

Villa San Valentino

Location Merano, Austria
Architects Stephen Unger Architects
Completion Date 2008
Site Area 200m²
Energy Consumption 46 kWh/m²a
Photos © Günther Stockklause,
Franz Dernt, Kurt Peintne

The site of Villa San Valentino is located in the named area, directly on those downhill curves, where the Adige valley opens into the Venosta valley. This explains, at first glance, the particular form of the double house that reproduces the curve of the downhill curves. Only at second glance you see the double curvature of the building.

Because the slope on which the villa was built is southern orientated, the location of the property is suitable especially to orient after the sun's path. The average angle of the sun on 21 June is a 46 ° angle and the angle of the building corresponds exactly to the curvature. Thus, the shape of the building has revealed as a hybrid, which is hosting the one hand, exposure to the sun and the other follows the course of regional landscape.

Furthermore, notice that the window openings of the curved south façade are relatively small, but the tilt of the façade is the optimal light yet given. The shape of these openings corresponds to the traditional pattern when working with shingles.

The larch shingles, which are unusual in this modern application of a contemporary villa, are known more by historical churches and castles. It is also already apparent that this traditional material is ideal for dynamic and three-dimensional curved shapes. So was the choice of architects, in addition to the request with regional materials and methods to work on this roof covering material. They applied 12cm shingles, which shall be the visible area of the shingle. They are arranged in three layers of scales and any shape is possible. The wood shingles are

1

handmade on the alpine tradition of craftsmanship and ten years dried. Over time they will set silvery patina and visually be reminiscent of stones; the life span – similar to the historic roofing – easily goes over a century.

The idea of sustainability is to be found in the consistent use of natural and locally available building materials. All materials are available in the region, including the interior. The local Lasa marble is in the bathrooms, granite and porphyry stone for floors, and oak, lime or smoked, for doors and wooden floors.

The south façade is built in wood-and-beam structure built of larch and the north wall consists of brick masonry. East and west solar-active mirror was used.

In the ceiling a solar-active heating and cooling system is integrated with two separate circuits for the two residential units.

1. West view © Günther Stockklause
2. South view: garden ©Gunther Stockklauser

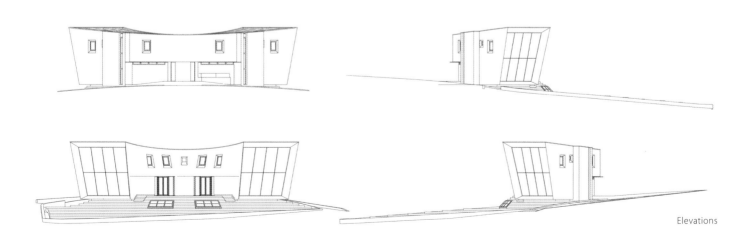

Elevations

Design Idea

3. North view: courtyard ©Gunther Stockklauser

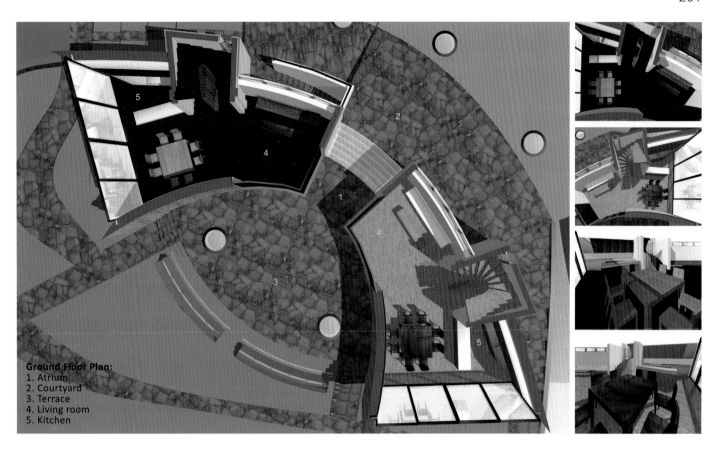

Ground Floor Plan:
1. Atrium
2. Courtyard
3. Terrace
4. Living room
5. Kitchen

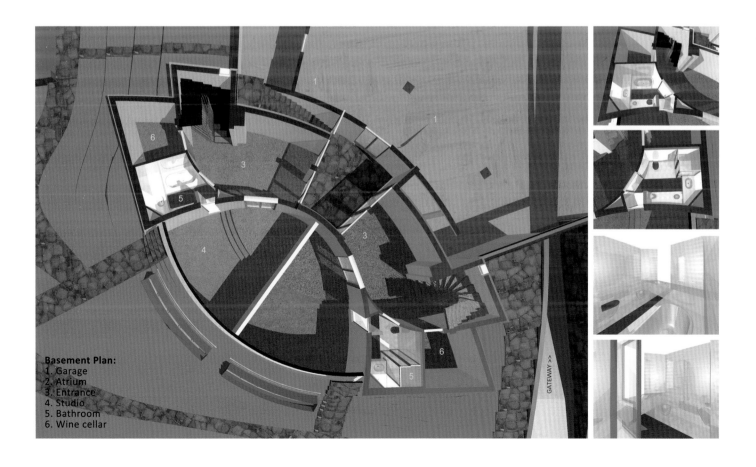

Basement Plan:
1. Garage
2. Atrium
3. Entrance
4. Studio
5. Bathroom
6. Wine cellar

GATEWAY >>

4

4. South-east view © Franz Derntl
5. Façade detail

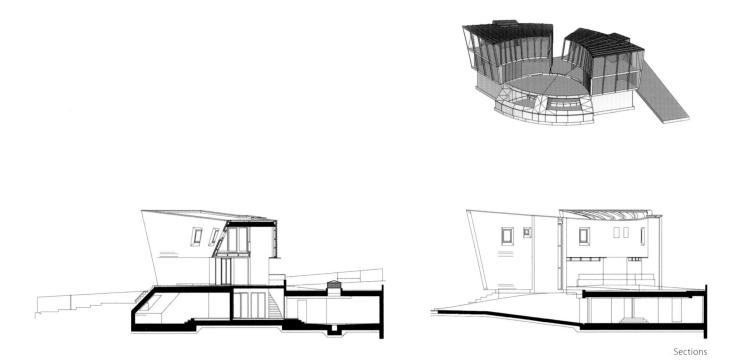

Sections

6

7

8

6. Kitchen © Franz Derntl
7. Dining room © Franz Derntl
8. Living room © Franz Derntl

N+C Townhouse

Location Geelong, Australia
Architects studio101 architects
Completion Date 2009
Area 256m^2
Photos © Trevor Mein (meinphoto)

Inspired by the traditional character weatherboard houses of the region, the N+C Residence is a new split level townhouse, custom designed for a local Geelong family. The site of only 400 square metres is located in an established residential area only minutes from the glorious Geelong waterfront. The architectural design reflects the owner's requirements for a sustainable, compact and low-maintenance home, full of fun, light and space. Functionally, the brief called for a continuous open plan spatial arrangement to maximise light and ventilation, three bedrooms, a mezzanine study and flexible off-street parking that could also double as an extended play space.

Located in a Council regulated heritage zone, the balancing of the owner's brief and the Town Planning requirements resulted in a restrained but exciting fusion of forms and materials that borrowed from the surrounding streetscape. The recycled timber skeletal structure that extends throughout the house was cut to length, lifted into position and bolted together like a life-size meccano set. The timber structure was then wrapped in a skin-like fashion with a traditional palette of materials including timber weatherboards, high-level glazing and red brick masonry to the service wing.

The unified client and architect relationship led to a wonderful refined and sustainable home, packed full of life and character while also respecting the traditional heritage streetscape.

The established character homes of the region provided inspiration for the forms and materials incorporated into the design concept. A traditional gable roof form was given a contemporary twist by extending the length along the

site, delicately floating above a ring of high level glazing. The roof then cantilevers and tapers to a fine edge at its extremities, proving high-level ventilation and winter sun penetration while also sun shading against the hot summer sun. The use of traditional materials and concealing the upper level within the gable roof space also contributes to the polite and respectful external appearance.

Internally, the design really unfolds providing a sensual sense of warmth and continuous spatial flow between the zones and levels. The simple rectilinear pavilion plan steps down the site following the natural topography with spaces linked by sliding walls, doors, louvres and mezzanine levels. A continuous timber walkway (recycled spotted gum) forms a central spine through the linear pavilion and links the internal and external spaces through a system of pivoting, sliding and louvered screens.

With the owners sharing a refined sustainable vision with the architects, a wide variety of ecologically sound design principals were incorporated into the project, including: Floor planning designed to maximise northern orientation to the living and play spaces; Thermal mass for internal heat storage is provided by the polished concrete floor slab – with in-slab thermostatically controlled hydronic heating; A central courtyard space allows cross ventilation and northern sun penetration deep into the central core of the house; Providing eaves and carefully considered cantilevered sun shading devices to welcome the winter sun but also shield from the hot summer sun; Maximising openable window sources to assist with cross ventilation throughout the home both in north/south and east/west axis; Openable high level louvre windows also provide for significant hot air exhaust and ventilation.

2

1. House viewed from the yard
2. House viewed from roadside

Sustainable Design (Below):
1. Winter sun
2. Summer sun
3. Cross-flow ventilation
4. High-level windows for heat escape in summer
5. Underground rainwater tanks
6. Thermal mass
7. Grey water recycling system
8. Low-E double glazed windows with argon gas
9. Fully insulated floors, walls, ceilings + roof

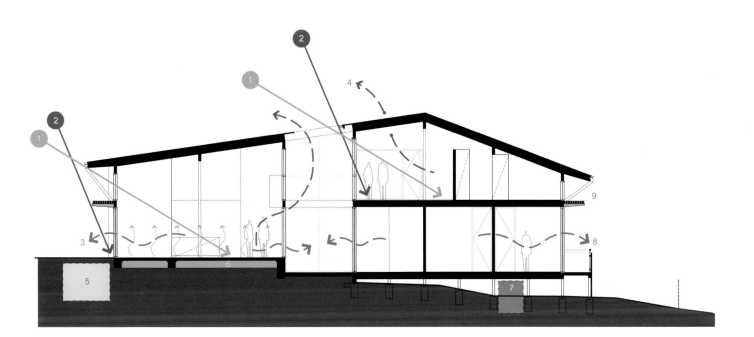

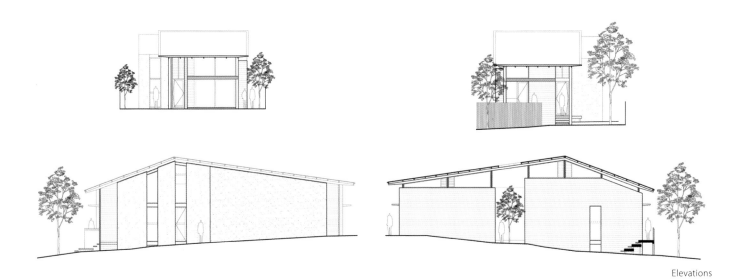

Elevations

3

3. Living room
4. Kitchen

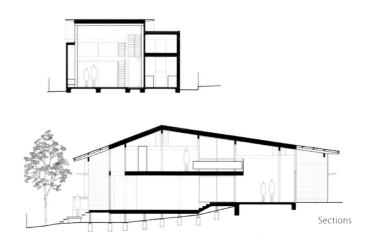

Sections

5

6

Ground Floor Plan and Sustainable Design:
A. Winter sun
B. Cross-flow ventilation
1. Living room
2. Dining
3. Kitchen
4. Bedroom
5. Bathroom
6. WC

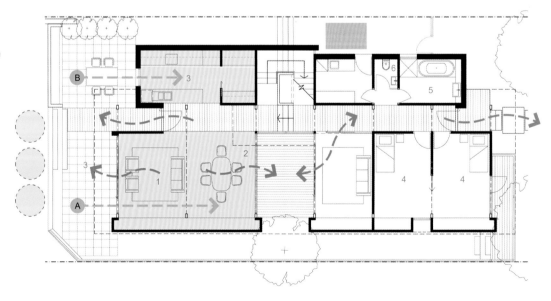

7

5. Study / work space
6. Corridor
7. Bedroom

Tiburon House

Location San Francisco, USA
Architects Andrea Ponsi Architetto
Completion Date 2008
Construction Area 850m^2
Photos © Richard Barnes

On San Francisco Bay, on the eastern side of Tiburon peninsula, at the end of a short road running steeply downhill amidst the vegetation, a narrow triangular valley slopes gently down to a little beach. The house is located in the centre of this valley and opens directly onto the beach, which in the course of the day widens and contracts with the rising and falling of the tide.

This would be a fitting name for this building, whose floor plan is the result of a movement of contraction and expansion in the direction of the four points of the compass, in search of a continuous relation between interior and exterior space.

The centre of the house is an empty space, a courtyard-garden surrounded by a glass-walled gallery along its perimeter. The wings of the house radiate out from this space towards the four cardinal points: four rectangular pavilions whose autonomy is accentuated by individual sloping copper roofs.

The pavilions hold the guest quarters, service areas and garage, master bedrooms, and living area. The living area opens, through a long wall of sliding glass doors, onto a wooden deck that descends gradually to the beach.

The whole building is conceived as a light structure nestled softly into the site. Its exterior skin is made up of a floating curtain wall of slats of "ipe" wood distanced from each other and detached from the walls behind them. This configuration creates a ventilated wall which contributes to the temperature control of the house.

Linearity is a recurring theme of the project. Besides the overall architectural layout, the linear development of the forms and space is repeated in the parallel lines of the wooden panelling on the exterior walls, the copper tubing sun-blinds in the gallery, the sliding panels of sheet aluminum, and the various objects and furnishings made to order for the project.

The custom-designed furnishings emphasise the use of copper. These include the big garage doors and the front door, some of the handles, the sun-blinds along the gallery, various lamps (vestibule, gallery, and kitchen) and an outdoor shower. All these elements were made by artisans in Italy. Copper is also used to cover all the roofs.

The house is completely autonomous in terms of energy. As an alternative to air conditioning, natural ventilation is ensured by the large sliding glass walls and the presence of the inner courtyard with its function of thermal compensation. The house also has a system of forced-air aspiration powered by the electricity produced by solar photovoltaic cells.

The building's electrical needs are fully furnished by about 100 square metres of solar photovoltaic panels mounted on the roofs and about 90 square metres of special "solar glass panels" consisting of photovoltaic foil sealed between two sheets of glass. These panels, mounted on various shelter-roofs along the building, function as protection for the pathways and sun-blinds for the south-facing walls.

Elevation

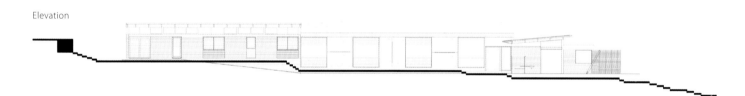

1. House viewed from yard
2. Overlooking copper roofs
3. Exterior detail
4. Terrace

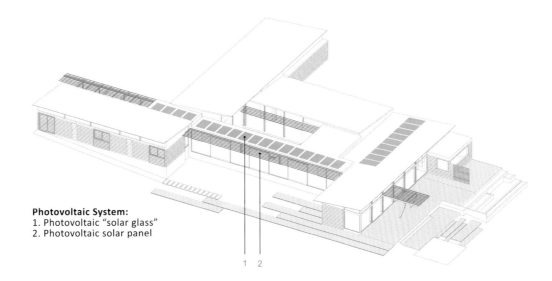

Photovoltaic System:
1. Photovoltaic "solar glass"
2. Photovoltaic solar panel

Passive Solar Gain:
1. Open patio
2. June 21
3. December 21

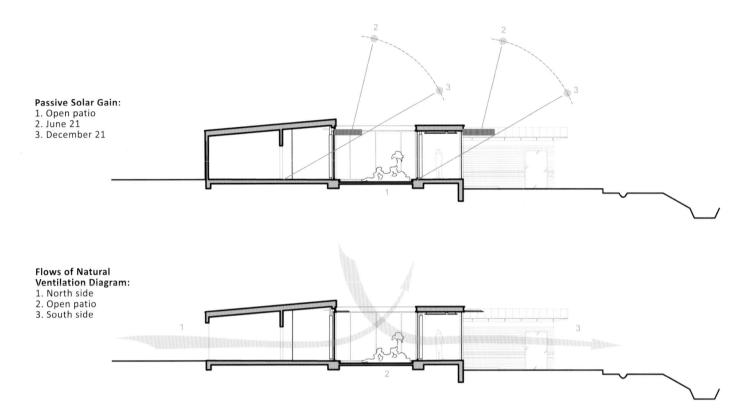

Flows of Natural Ventilation Diagram:
1. North side
2. Open patio
3. South side

5. Exterior detail
6,8. Corridor
7. Rotary wood door
9. Outdoor shower

10

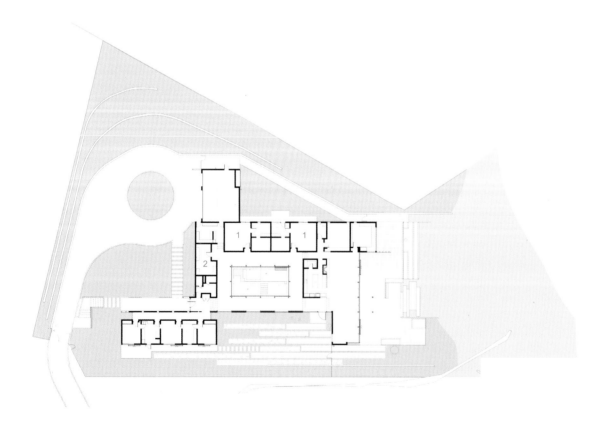

House Plan:
1. Bedroom
2. Kitchen

10. Kitchen viewed from living room
11. Living room

Twisted Corner

Location Leiden, the Netherlands
Architects Sophie Valla architects
in collaboration with Marc Koelher
Completion Date 2010
Photos © Luuk Kramer

The urban development defined by the city of Leiden offered a special strategy: a solution in-between mass production and customised villa. The aim was to create the quality of an individual house within a collective urban block.

The master plan obliged each private owner to build the project together with the neighbours of the same block. This led to a greater efficiency for the structural system and for the building site management.

This resulted in: 20 privates houses, planned and designed by 20 different architects for 20 private clients. Yet, it was all engineered with only one structural advisor, one building services advisor and built with one main contractor.

Still the designers could express identity by applying different materials for the façade and proposing different volumes. This strategy helped maintaining a great variation for each house while gaining the advantages of mass production. This is a very good time and cost-effective solution in comparison to construction of single detached individual houses.

Twisted Corner provides living between the park and the terraces. The form of the building responds to the light and views conditions to create a comfortable internal environment. In a sense, it has been designed inside out. The east-façade openings are directing the views to the future park into front while long vertical openings, on the north façade bring enough light in the spaces without the interior being exposed. Similar openings are used

1

for the bedrooms and bathroom on the first floor. The house was designed with emphasis on effective energy management and sustainable technologies. All windows have high isolation HR++ double glass (high performance glazing). The district heating is a system distributing heat generated in a centralised location.

The EPDM single-ply rubber roofing membrane provides durable and low impact roofing solution. The balanced ventilation system introduces and exhausts approximately equal quantities of fresh outside air and polluted inside air, respectively. It facilitates good distribution of fresh air by placing supply and exhaust vents in appropriate places. The balanced ventilation system is designed to supply fresh air to bedrooms and living rooms where people spend the most time.

The façade is built with use of environmental friendly materials. The prefabricated wooden frame panels and wooden window frames are environmental friendly materials. Most of the components were chosen with emphasis on the maximum efficiency of the material use (the cladding panels) and prefabrication. For the cladding panels, the designers searched for the maximum efficiency of material use, with no waste of material when cut from the original panels.

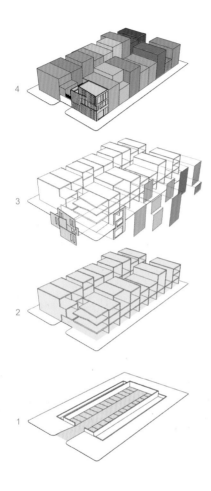

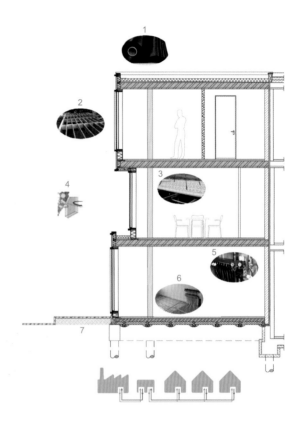

Eco Development Strategy:
1. Half-sunken parking garage
2. Collective construction:
   prefabricated elements
3. Individual construction:
   prefabricated façade
4. Mass produced urban block
   with customised houses

Energy Management:
1. EPDM on the roof
2. Prefabricated wooden frame panels
3. Prefabricated concrete floor
4. HR++ glass
5. Balanced ventilation
6. Under-floor heating
7. District heating

Longitudinal Elevation::
1. Cladding: Eternit Natura panels
2. HR++ glass
3. Colorbel, emailled glass
4. Safety glass
5. Aluminium
6. Metal fence
7. Aluminium parapet
8. Wooden door
9. Sliding door
10. Garage door

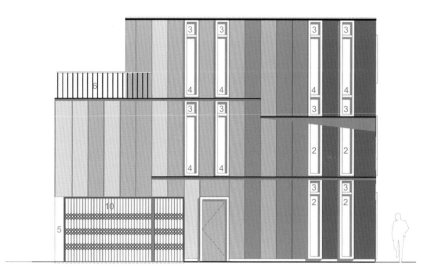

1. Side view
2. View from backyard
3. Living room viewed from kitchen
4. Kitchen and stair viewed from living room
5. Bathroom

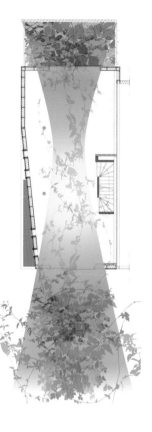
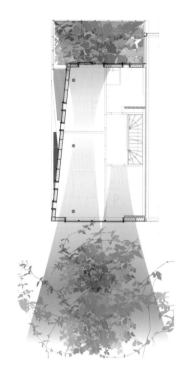

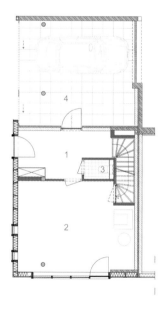
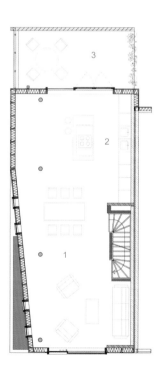
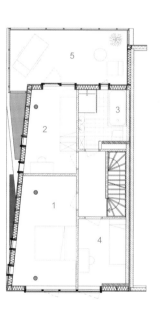

Ground Floor Plan:
1. Entrance hall
2. Playroom
3. Toilet
4. Garage

First Floor Plan:
1. Living room
2. Open kitchen
3. Terrace

Second Floor Plan:
1. Master bedroom
2. Bedroom
3. Bathroom
4. Baby room
5. Terrace

Casa en el Bosqu

Location Estado de Mexico, Mexico
Architects Parque Humano
Completion Date 2009
Construction Area 650m^2
Photos © Paul Rivera, ArchPhoto
Award Silver medal, Mexico Architecture Biennale 2008

The site is a splendid plot covering 3,500 square metres with rich and varied flora, very tall trees, and a view towards the layered hills of Valle de Bravo – a town 150 km south-west of Mexico City. The climate is cool in winter (-2°C) while summer temperatures can reach 33°C, heavy rain falls daily between June and October.

The house occupies a natural ledge in the hillside, facing the view to the south and turning its back to the winds coming in from the north. The ground drops away beneath the floor, emphasising the slope of the land and thereby dramatising the house's progress through the site. The house evokes the feeling of floating above the garden, accentuating a sense of contact with nature.

Two pavilions, unequal in size, are set in front of the pool area. The first and biggest one contains the living and dining spaces, kitchen and a working studio. The second one: two bedrooms. Each pavilion was carefully placed on the site, incorporating all the existing trees into the programme and facing the most important views. The house is deeply rooted in the existing landscape.

Upon arrival, the visitor encounters several experiences: the escarpment, the flora, the house, the reflecting pool. Visitors are received under the protection of a steel enclosure, entering through a small door that leads to the living room, thereby emphasising the contrast between the closed nature of the entrance and the full openness of the living spaces and the valley itself.

1

The continuity between landscape and building is stressed by a glazed structural window system, transcending conventional distinctions between inside and outside. As a result, all the spaces are in direct and intimate contact with the outdoors.

The cladding of the house evolved progressively in order to fit into the context of the town. An artisanal clay veneer was specially developed for the project, similar in texture to the traditional houses that you notice in the area. Its reaction to the weather causes the material to change constantly in response to varying levels of humidity.

The concept of sustainability was addressed not only in technical aspects but also in the relationship that the house keeps with its immediate environment, the

lightness of the impact on the ground and the mimesis with it. The design of the house has been directed to respect nature and to establish a connection with the place.

The architects used local, renewable materials with recycled content and low emission, such as certified wood and stone, both of local origin. Rainwater is captured and stored, grey water reuse, and solar panels generate most of the energy the home needs. The house rests on a natural curve of the slope; its elevation offers expansive views of the lake and mountains.

Large floor-to-ceiling windows facing south receive the sun's heat in winter, while the angled roof overhangs provide shade for the summer sun. Cross

2

ventilation in the interiors is natural due to the flexibility of opening of the house.

The designers developed a special piece of clay with natural insulating properties for the coating, similar to those used for traditional houses in the area. These blocks are located on the north side and work as a protection from strong winds from the north.

No tree was removed during the construction of the house, and many were incorporated into the design to highlight the connection and respect for nature.

1. House and surroundings
2. View towards studio
3. East elevation
4. View towards bedrooms pavilion

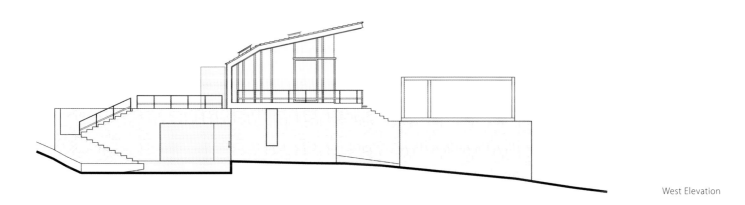

West Elevation

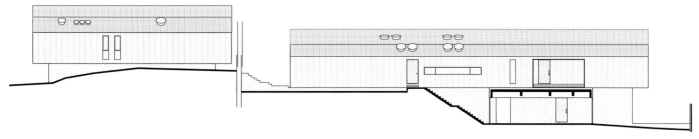

North Elevation

5. Entrance court
6. Entrance court & fountain
7. House and pool overview

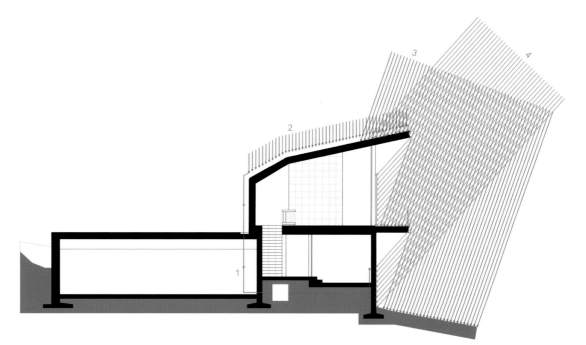

Bioclimatic Performance:
1. Rain water tank
2. Rain water
3. Summer solstice 70°
4. Winter solstice 47°

8

8. Living room
9. Living room on the upper floor

9

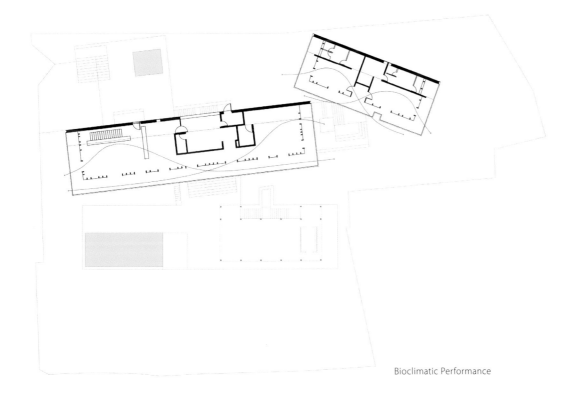

Bioclimatic Performance

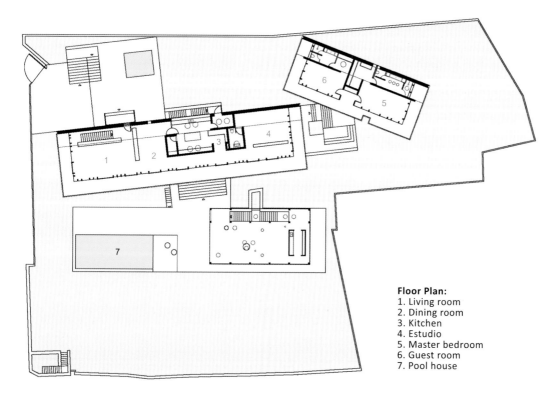

Floor Plan:
1. Living room
2. Dining room
3. Kitchen
4. Estudio
5. Master bedroom
6. Guest room
7. Pool house

11

10. Master bedroom
11. Bathroom

New Building to House Oirschot

Location Oirschot, the Netherlands
Architects Toon Bullens Architect
Completion Date 2008
Construction Area 275m^2
Photos © James van Leuven

The focus of the house is the view, the garden and the wind corridor for the nearby windmill. By sitting the sleeping area partially underground, where the temperature is almost constant, this area requires minimal heating or cooling. The north-facing street side is virtually closed whereas the south-facing garden side is totally open. The glass curtain wall on the garden side is recessed in a frame and has movable (automatic) and fixed exterior sun blinds. In summer, the blinds exclude inconvenient sun; in winter, the desirable sun is used to generate passive solar energy.

The use of a ground source heat pump to provide heating, hot water and cooling makes the energy management sustainable and the house extremely comfortable.

The house is ventilated by a balanced ventilation system with high-efficiency (95%) heat recovery. The steel trusses provide flexibility to adapt the interior to changing situations, trends, and individual requirements. The floors and walls are made of recyclable concrete or stone-based materials.

Durable natural slate shingles on the roof and side walls and western red cedar facing on the front are mounted on FSC-certified timber backing and insulated with mineral wool. The low-maintenance aluminium curtain walls have high-grade insulating glazing.

By storage in the ground, terrestrial heat can be converted into warm or cold water, which is used for heating and cooling via pipes in the floors. The

use of passive solar energy reduces the energy consumption for heating significantly. Fresh air from outside is pre-warmed before it enters the house. By placing the exhaust air valves in the ridge (warm air rises), an incoming fresh air temperature of 23°C is measured in winter, with an outside temperature of -10°C. Rain-water is returned to the ground by permeation.

This house is an outstanding example of a design that responds to the surroundings while using sustainable energy-saving measures that arise naturally from the design.

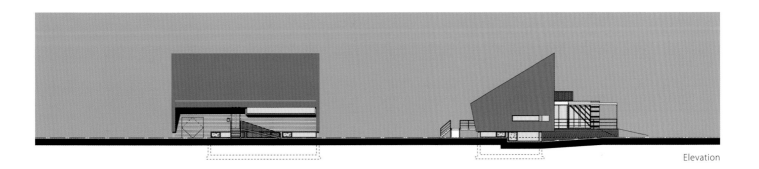

Elevation

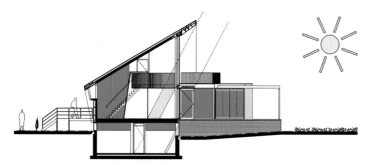

Highest Sun Position (Summer) 21st, June vs. Sunblind

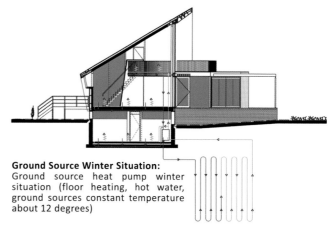

Ground Source Winter Situation:
Ground source heat pump winter situation (floor heating, hot water, ground sources constant temperature about 12 degrees)

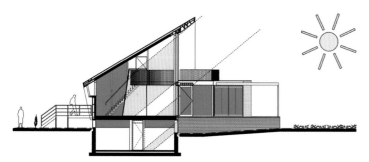

Midyear Sun Position vs. Sunblind (Sun Position 21st, March – 21st, September)

Ground Source Summer Situation:
Ground source heat pump summer situation (floor heating, hot water, ground sources constant temperature about 12 degrees)

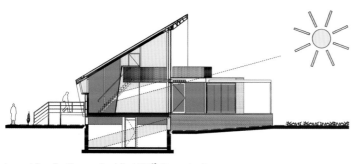

Lowest Sun Position vs. Sunblind (21st, December)

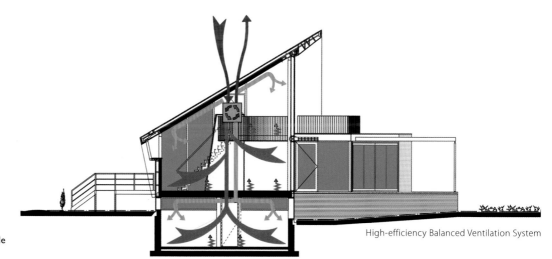

1. General view from the waterside
2. Side view

High-efficiency Balanced Ventilation System

3

3. North façade
4. Outdoor gathering area

4

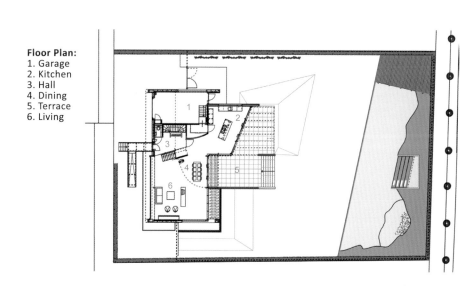

Floor Plan:
1. Garage
2. Kitchen
3. Hall
4. Dining
5. Terrace
6. Living

7

5. Bar and kitchen viewed from the outside
6. Kitchen
7. Living room

York Street Social Housing

Location Dublin, Ireland

Architects Seán Harrington Architects

Completion Date 2009

Gross Floor Area 5,600m²

Site Area 2,300m²

Photos © Philip Lauterbach, Sasfi Hope Ross, Ines Billings

The building wraps round a south-facing courtyard and is designed to benefit from controlled passive solar gain using glazed winter gardens and solar thermal roof panels. It also has an energy-efficient communal heating system, and energy loss is minimised by smaller openings on north-facing elevations and high levels of insulation everywhere. Rainwater from the roofs is collected and stored to irrigate the garden and allotments, and for car washing. Great emphasis has been placed on communal facilities such as community meeting rooms, a shared garden, a children's play area, and recycling facilities including a communal waste composter.

Sheep's wool thermal insulation is used in the timber frame dwellings. Roofs are made from reclaimed floor joists. The use of cement is minimised, with natural lime render and mortar and concrete is made from

GGBS "green" cement. Natural linoleum floor finishes are used and there is no PVC or MDF.

Most of the roofs are covered in sedum, retaining storm water and encouraging bio-diversity. Rainwater is collected in water butts and used for garden irrigation.

Recycling and composting is encouraged, with sorting bins in each kitchen. There is a communal organic food composter which processes food and plant waste, turning it into compost over a four-week period. This is used in the courtyard, the roof gardens or on individual balcony planters or pots.

There are a resident's vegetable allotment and fruit trees in the courtyard. Accessible roof terraces allow for vegetables to be grown in wooden planter boxes.

1

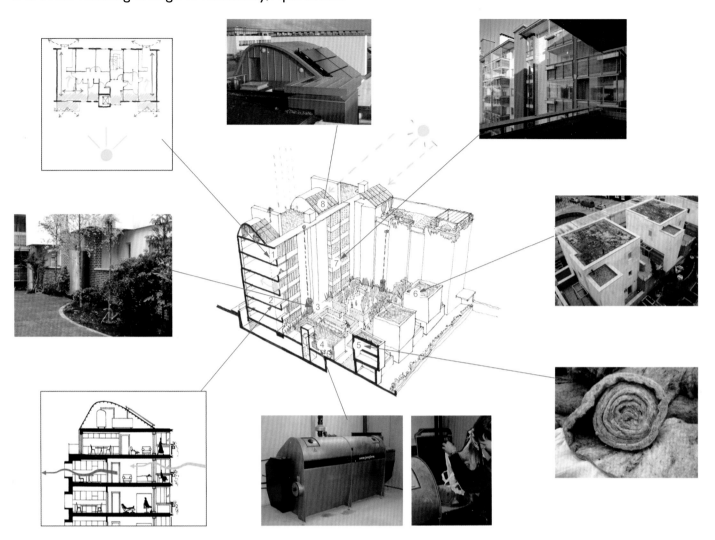

Environmental Diagram:
1. Living spaces face south over the communal gardens, while kitchens face north over the street
2. Apartments are naturally ventilated through opening windows on the north and south walls
3. Rainwater harvesting for watering the gardens and washing cars
4. An anaerobic digester in the recycling centre located in the communal gardens
   convert kitchen waste into compost for the garden and window boxes.
5. Natural materials: sheep's wool thermal insulation in timber frame construction
6. Sedum green roof reduce rainwater run-off and encourage bio-diversity
7. South-facing balconies with glass shutters enable year-round use and act as solar collectors
8. Solar thermal roof panels for heating and hot water

1. Building viewed from street
2. Façade
3. Building and surroundings

4. Windows with stained glass
5. Balcony
6. Living room
7. Kitchen and dining area

6

7

Greenon19 Townhouse

Location Santa Monica, USA
Architects Jesse Bornstein Architecture
Completion Date 2008
Construction Area 690m^2
Photos © Bernard Wolf

This architect-driven 5-unit townhouse development occupies a typical infill site within the City of Santa Monica's semi-urban grid. Its modern design, with integrated green technologies and materials, is a significant departure from the traditionally based neighbourhood context.

With its serial pattern and clean dipartite formal composition capped with semi-transparent bi-facial photovoltaic solar canopies that provide shade for roof decks as well as over 3,000 Kwh electricity generation per year for each unit, these townhouses are designed to incite excitement and a sense of optimism for a sustainable future.

Other hallmarks of the project include a simple palette of sustainable materials inside and out, an abundance of natural light and ventilation, and connections to outdoor spaces on each level.

The project's system technologies minimise adverse environmental impact. The lighting system makes extensive use of fluorescents and LEDs.

Water conserving features include low flow plumbing equipment and fixtures, 100% drought-tolerant landscaping and drip irrigation. All rainwater is retained on site for irrigation use and urban runoff mitigation. HVAC equipment exceeds 90% efficiency and uses non-toxic refrigerant.

Among the project's many other sustainable technologies and materials are minimalist, double-sided, ethanol-fueled fireplaces set in custom FSC-

certified bamboo casework. These central hearths for the 21st century generate a cool ambience while effectively warming each unit's entire two-storey primary volume.

Developed, designed, and constructed with pride, passion and environmental sensitivity, these one-of-a-kind modern, custom-crafted townhouses comprise the first green-built development in Santa Monica.

Greenon19 is the recipient of Santa Monica's Sustainable Quality Award and the EPA's Energy Star Home Rating and has been the subject of articles in local, regional and international press as well as several TV newscasts and architectural home tours.

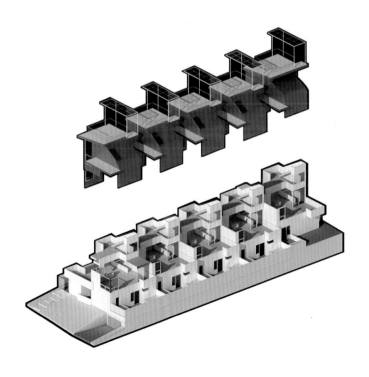

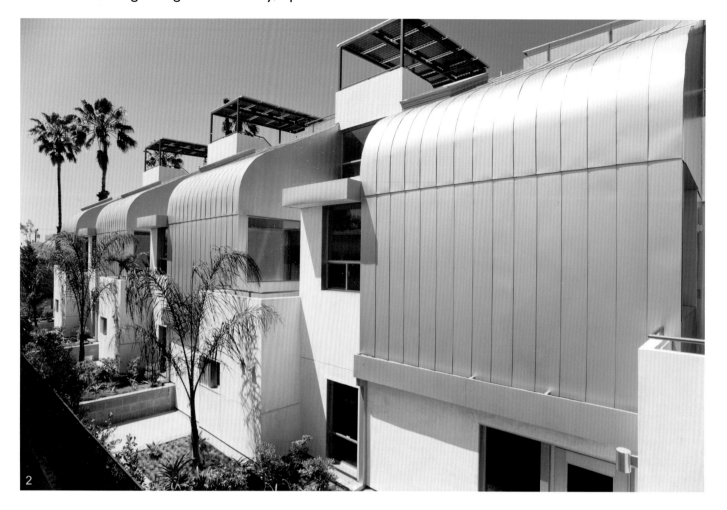

1. Side view
2. Sheet metal panel cladding
3. Bi-facial photovoltaic solar canopies
4. Front view
5. Solar canopy

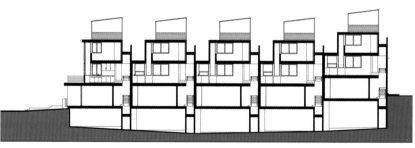

Section

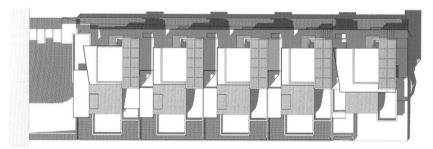

Master Plan

Eco Diagram (Below):
1. Translucent photovoltaic solar canopies shade roof deck and generate over 3,000 kWh per year for each unit
2. North-facing window glass systems for daylight / ventilation
3. Operable solar glass skylight for natural light / ventilation
4. On-site rain water retension for irrigation and urban runoff mitigation
5. Structural concrete slab floor as "Solar Tank"
6. 100% drought-tolerant landscape with drip irrigation

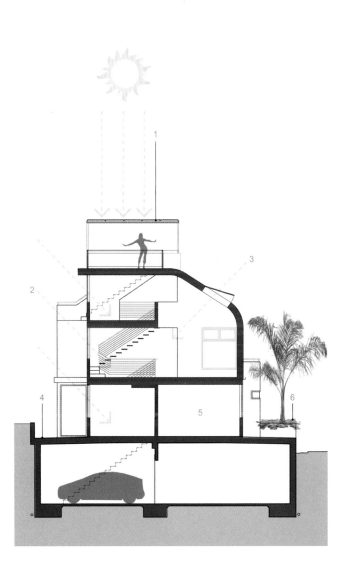

6,7. Living room
8. General view of living room

8

Floor Plan:
1. Master room
2. Bedroom
3. Patio
4. Kitchen/Dining
5. Living
6. Deck

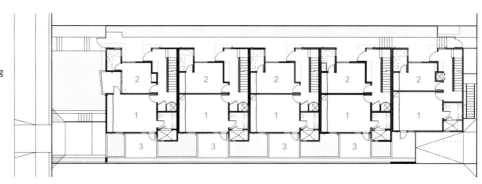

123 Social Housing Apartments in Vallecas

Location Madrid, Spain
Architects Somosarquitectos / Luis Burriel Bielza,
Pablo Fernandez Lewicki, Jose Antonio Tallon Iglesias
Completion Date 2009
Construction Area 14,934m^2
Site Area 1,318m^2
Photos © ARQUITECTOS

The project raises eight floors above the ground along one of the limits of the block imposed by the restrained urban planning. The great scale of the building forces it to act as a visual screen for the green area that stands aside, physically protecting from the twelve-lane road on the opposite side. The volume, specifically fixed according to the rigid city-planning rules to obtain the highest amount of apartments asked by the public developer, drove the architects to respect the enveloped volume determined in the planning, using other tools to establish a dialogue with the surrounding urbanscape. Thus, the façade and its surface remains as one of the most powerful instruments to manipulate the perceptive scale.

The ground floor is a delicate area, as it must deal with the street, separating car and pedestrian entrances. The apartments on this floor are oriented towards the so-called green area and they have been raised two metres from street level in order to provide them with some extra isolation from the view of the possible passer-by. The official façade opens towards the hustle and bustle common of a commercial street with heavy traffic. It gathers the commercial premises and the three accesses (parking in and out and pedestrian). Even though the number of apartments demanded two separated accesses, the architects decided to create a single welcome space which would be big enough to interact with the scale of the building.

This hall area is completely open on both sides and its rectangular shape establishes a dialogue with the free-form platforms of the mailbox area. Thus, the entrance

1

is modulated by means of generous terraces finished with vitreous mosaic, prepared for the installation of the mailboxes, which grow in height emphasising the landing as a highly compressed space. These transitions of scale are unified through a green ceiling completely illuminated with the so-called network of protruding lights-skylight.

For accessing every residential unit the designers rescue an ancient scheme developed in the XVI century in Madrid called "corralas". It is based in the use of an inner court which allows for effective crossed ventilation for each apartment. A single extra-wide entry hall lets fresh air enter this vertical shaft. Each unit is divided into a "dry" area comprising bedrooms and living room, and a "wet" area comprising kitchen, bathroom and drying room. The first one opens onto the polycarbonate façade and the other opens onto the inner court.

Solar power covers 80% of energy consumption to heat water for everyday use. The polycarbonate skin provides extra insulation values, whether they might be acoustic and thermal.

The architects employ 40-millimetres thick open-celled extruded polycarbonate panels with seven internal walls and six air chambers, protected against U.V. rays.

Furthermore, this building is 100% recyclable, uses a low amount of energy on manufacturing and transportation; it has a high degree of purity; and it features a high degree as well of industrialisation in production and assembly.

Eco - section

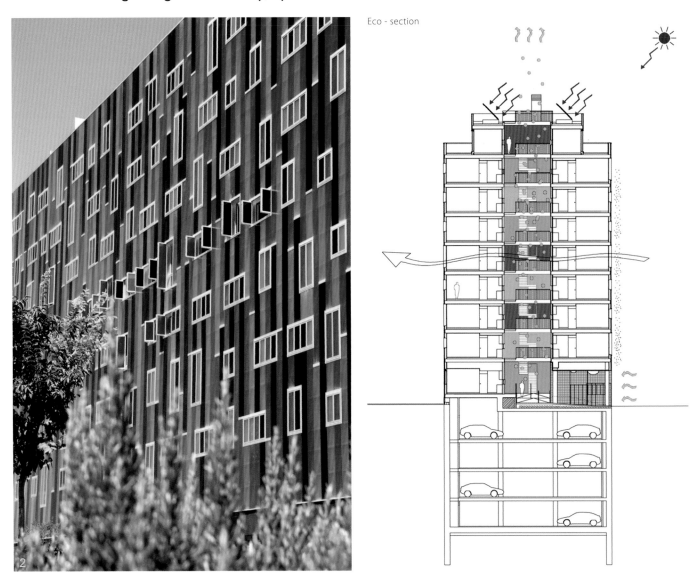

1. General view of building
2-4. Façade window detail

5

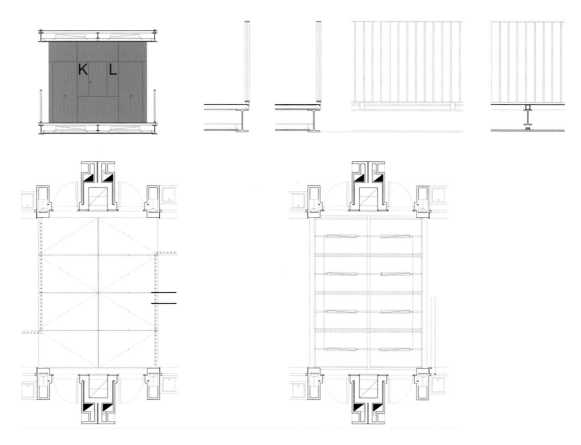

5,6. Internal corridor and staircase connecting each floor

7

7. Entrance lobby
8. Mail box in the entrance lobby

Floor Plan:
1. Main entrance
2. Secondary access
3. Garage access
4. Hall
5. Interior courtyard
6. Commercial area

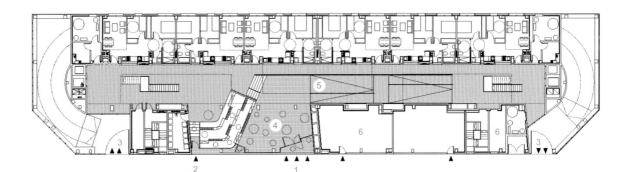

Urban Lake Houses

Location Largo San Giorgio, Italy
Architects C+S Associati
Completion Date 2010
Construction Area 11,000m²
Photos © Alessandra Bello and Luca Casonato

A path sews together the lake, the park and the square of San Giorgio church, creating a public open space facing the new housing and the church. The buildings mould themselves with the lake boundaries and their elevations are designed by big wooden windows which both reflect the landscape and bring it inside the houses' sitting-rooms.

The plaster surfaces of the buildings, light grey and light ochre coloured, are on the same flush of the stone and, as an effect of the buildings' folds, one couldn't easily tell whether the slight differences of the chromatic effetcts are those of a colour or simply of the shadow.

The buildings grow with the levels of the paths surrounding the lake, forming a new urban connection whcih specifically changes material: Prun stone on the square, larch wood on the bridges crossing the lake and ochre concrete on the paths of the park. The path following the lake leaves the earth and jumps in the water with a metal structure suspended on sloping metal pillars. The volumes facing the square host the spaces of the church services.

Detailed architectural design defines also the other public parts of the buildings: entrance halls and public stairs, which are made of red-coloured wood, the auditorium (partially dag in the ground), with grey and red acoustic panels, the church classrooms which are graphically designed. All these spaces are naturally enlighted and enjoy views of the marvellous landscape of the lake outside. All the houses are opened to the lake with large wooden windows and sliding wood panels to darken the spaces inside.

The idea of sustainability of the project is to gather the local community around a lake and a new square, regaining a part of the town which was lost and preserving the memory of Pordenone town scale. The buildings are bent, following the lake layout so as to underline the importance of water. The lake itself becomes a contemporary source of energy as it exchanges heat with heat pumps. In this way the complex has no energy consumption.

The materials used for the project are local materials such as wood and stone, which has been used for the windows, the structural parts and final surfaces of the floors. Wood was used also outside in the landscape project as the paths around the lake and the bridges floors are made of larch. The square and the lower parts of the façades are made of Piasentina stone which is also a local material.

Together with the local materials used, natural resources of the project is very important also from the energetic point of view. In this case, the lake itself is not only the expression of the landscape of Pordenone, which is a very beautiful small historical town in the Northeast of Italy, built on the boundaries of the river Noncello, but it becomes also the energetic source. Urban Lake Houses are designed with a innovative heating and cooling pump system of pumps that exploits the constant temperature of the lake's water. In this way the pond is once more part of its contemporary surrounds, an energy provider for its community and a source of human inspiration.

1. General view of waterside building
2. Building surroundings
3. Side view of building

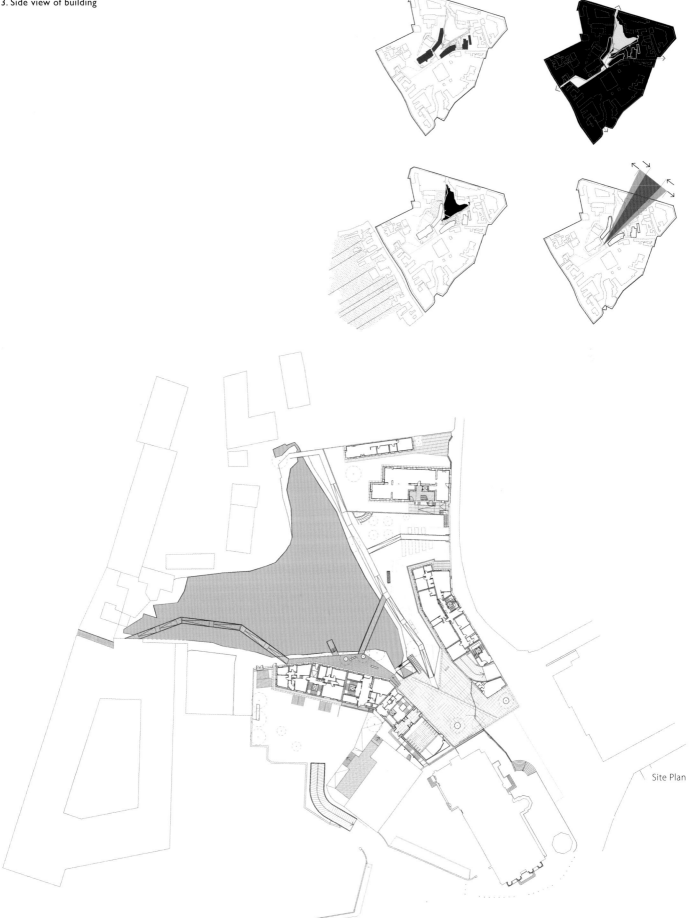

Site Plan

4,5. View from courtyard

Elevation

Section

Section

6-7. Garden landscaping with water feature

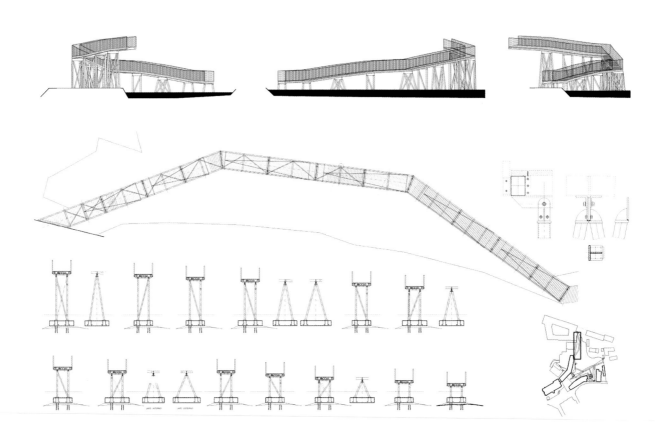

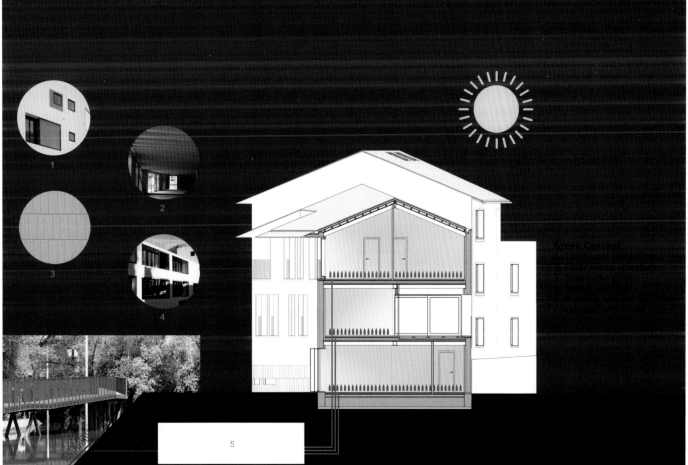

8

P7. Block 20 Dwellings and Shops

Location Barcelona, Spain
Architects narch/Joan Ramon Pascuets and Mònica Mosset
Completion Date 2008
Construction Area 2,500m^2
Photos © Hisao Suzuki

The building consists of dwellings, a three-storey commercial premises and the basement with 31 parking spaces and 20 storage rooms. A front light during the day, rich with dynamic volumes and shadows at night lights up as sifted light box, getting the building porous, light and various due to the use of light by its inhabitants, creating reflections, shadows and silhouettes that flow between interior and exterior.

A thin perforated leather, a translucent veil from the outside, works as a sunscreen for the proper functioning Meoro climate of the building, and as a visual filter to preserve the privacy of their occupants. From within the contrast in brightness between the pierced and the opaque panels manages to create a unique visual effect.

The dwellings are arranged around the central core of communications, leaving all stays in façade and all services inside. The location of the living-rooms in the corner can play with the composition of the façade featuring balconies on either side free and making it disappear on the four planes of enclosure.

Sliding system is applied throughout the building from the front where the shutter is replaced by panels of perforated plates to the inner divisions that are integrated sliding doors by Krona. The spatial flexibility, freedom of movement and distribution creates a clean, smooth and flexible space, expanding and extending spatial relationship.

1

400 panels and perforated aluminium sheet (3mm anodised matte silver, form the second skin of the building, creating an appearance with intangible boundaries and porous architecture that becomes imperceptible.

The panels slide along the entire façade, generating mobility uniformity in the front from the outside, while from inside the panels can come and go as needed, forming a front open system varies according to users and not determined by the architect.

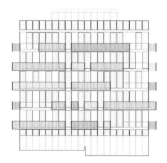
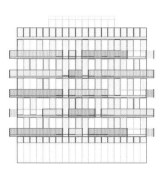
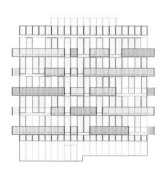
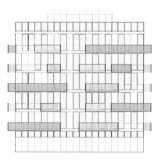

Elevations

1. Building viewed from street
2. General view of building

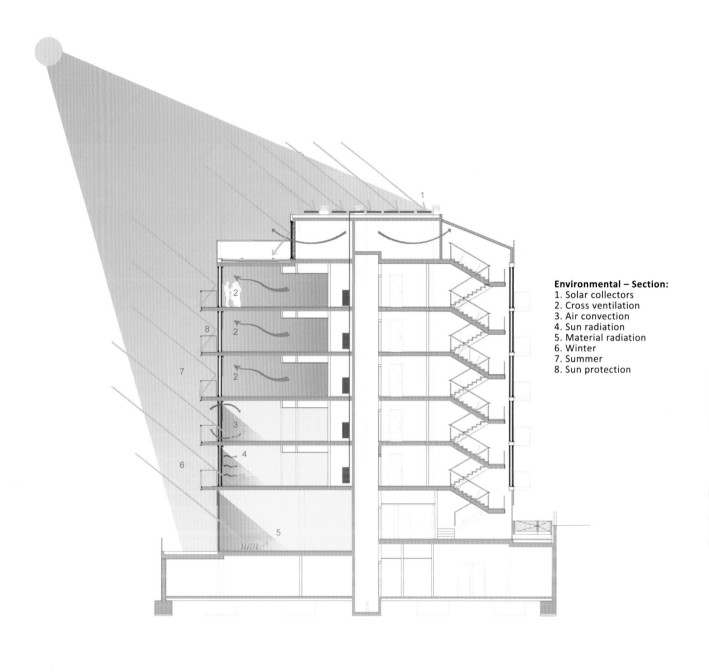

Environmental – Section:
1. Solar collectors
2. Cross ventilation
3. Air convection
4. Sun radiation
5. Material radiation
6. Winter
7. Summer
8. Sun protection

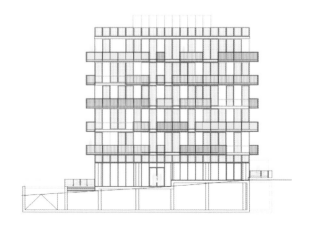

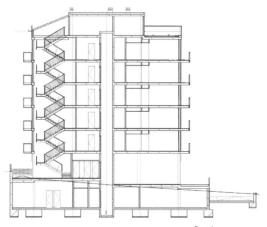

Sections

3,4. Façade detail
5. Interior detail

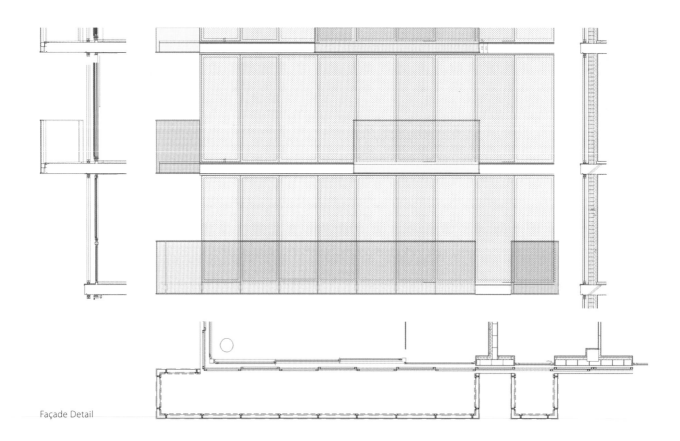

Façade Detail

5

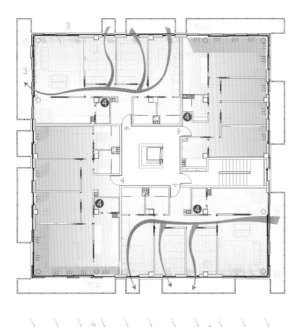

Floor Plan

Environmental – Section:
1. Summer
2. Winter
3. Sun protection
4. Water from solar panels

Block 30 Dwellings in Manresa

Location Barcelona, Spain
Architects narch / Joan Ramon Pascuets and Mònica Mosset
Completion Date 2009
Construction Area 4,500m²
Photos © Hisao Suzuki

The building is organised by two communication centres that serve two and three apartments per floor. To achieve this layout, there are two typologies, one oriented north-south with bathrooms in the centre and the other one faced to one façade with water area located inside. The first one has cross ventilation through opposite fronts, while the second one also have transverse ventilation with perpendicular façades.

The main feature is the large amount of natural light thanks to the generous dimensions of the balconies as well as the provision of access to the terrace from any room. The bathroom, situated in the centre, have two entrances to connect to different bedrooms and allows constant movement and crossed views and ventilation from north to south.

Since the building is located in a continental climate marked by contrasts in temperature between day and night and summer and winter, and conditioned by the orientation from west to east, the architects considered protecting and isolating the fronts north, east and west, while leverage and distribute strong energy gains from the south to the interior.

The main strategy was on one hand to achieve energy from the south façade and on the other hand to spread the gains in all rooms. The south façade was provided by a gallery comprised of a fully double glazed sliding skin, the inner and outer transparent translucent façades system, adaptable, flexible and multifunctional. A second skin of 5+5mm laminated glass translucent in south façade works as a thermal skin in winter and sunscreen in summer.

In winter daytime outdoor slides open to let in solar radiation heating the concrete mass with high thermal inertia, and close at night by irradiating the mass, which in turn is enhanced by heating under-floor water. In summer the outdoor runners close and open the interior while at the same time the exterior windows of the north façade are open getting natural cross ventilation.

A good insulation of solid parts, the thermal break in all woodwork including window frames, pillars, along with the generation of hot sanitary water with solar panels in the roof, minimises energetic consumption. The insulation of the separating walls between entities and between the rooms in the same housing guarantees the rest and the conviviality.

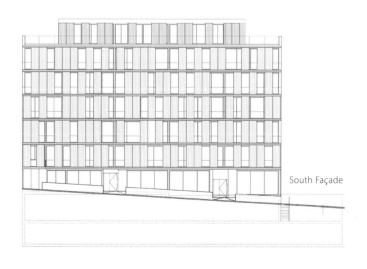

South Façade

1. General view
2. Façade night view
3. Side view

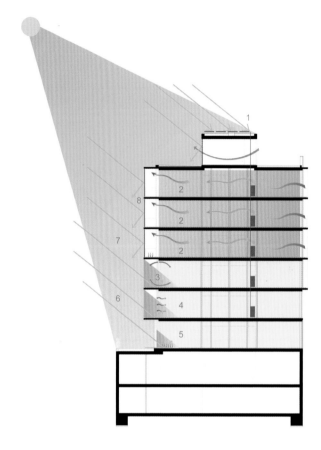

Section Diagram:
1. Flat solar collectors
2. Cross ventilation
3. Air convection
4. Solar radiation
5. Material radiation
6. Winter
7. Summer
8. Sun protection

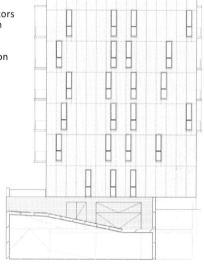

Floor Diagram:
1. Cavity wall
2. Sun protection
3. Sun radiation
4. Cross ventilation
5. Water from
   solar panels
6. Summer
7. Winter

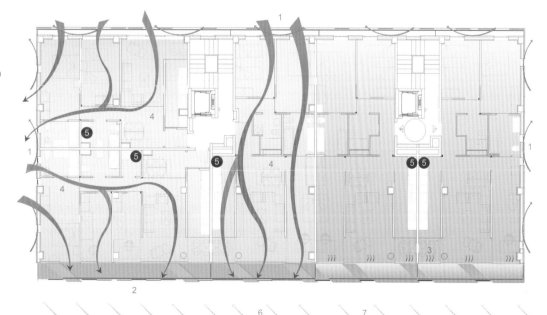

4-6. Interior detail

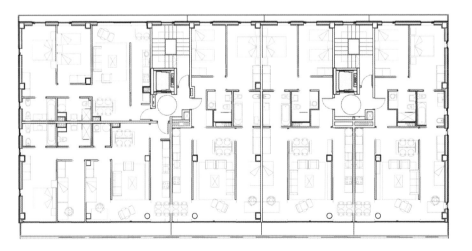

Floor Plan

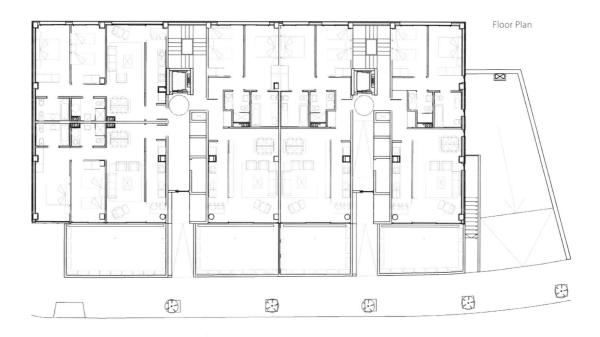

Floor Plan

H&E Housing

Location Paris, France
Architects David Elalouf Architecte
Completion Date 2008
Construction Area 7,260m²
Photos © Stephan Lucas, David Elalouf

This is a pilot operation in Paris in terms of Environmental Quality and Sustainable Development. Particular attention was paid to ways to reduce consumption of all order: water, heating, electricity, by implementing a high performance envelope. Along the same lines, the energy choices made allow reducing expenses, and a quality residential which provides for a more ecological approach habitat in the city.

The measures implemented include, in particular: a highly efficient insulation of façades, solar panels on the roof, forced-air mechanical ventilation that controls the air quality inside apartments, recovery of rainwater from terraces for irrigation and green roofs. On the ground floor, gardens in the ground promote absorption of rainwater. Furthermore, buildings are accessible at street level despite uneven topography

of the site; A "Green User's Guide", given to each inhabitant, helps the user in terms of sustainable development to initiate a participatory approach.

On the edge of the Rue de la Chapelle (historical axis of the Cardo of the Roman city), the two plots are located on both sides of the Impasse du Gué. The Impasse du Gué was enlarged to 18 metres (8 metres initially), initiating a new urban development in North Eastern Paris. It serves two plots: two buildings are located on the south grounds at the corner of Rue de la Chapelle, and two other buildings are located to the north.

The impasse is composed like a garden in the heart of the project, planted with magnolias and bamboo, it extends laterally with galleries on the ground floor

Sustainability Diagram:
1. Solar water heating panels
2. Air treatment
3. External wall insulation
4. Forced-air mechanical ventilation
5. Double-oriented flat
6. Watering
7. Solar hot water
8. Rainwater tank
9. Soil porosity
10. Ground Garden
11. Green roof

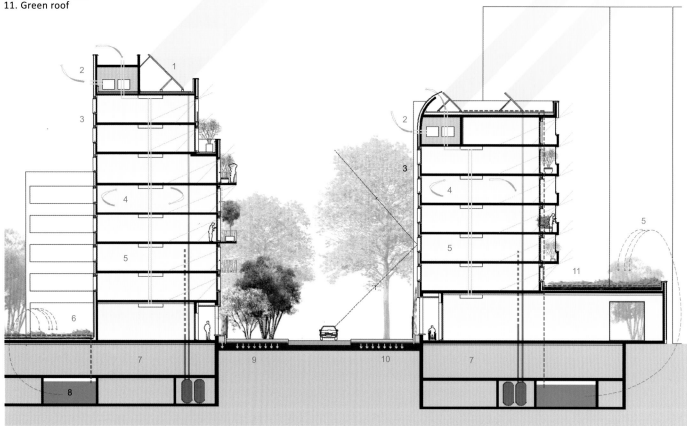

of buildings. Between the two buildings on the south side of the impasse, a coloured gap lets light in from south. It echoes the one located at the north.

The implementation of a "smart" and efficient envelope enables to reduce consumption of all kinds. Depending on their position relative to urban areas or cardinal orientation, the façades are covered with specific cladding materials: white polished concrete facing the street, fiber cement siding or aluminum cladding inside the plot. Smooth façades to north and east, with sets of reflectors deflect the solar rays inside the apartments.

The majority of dwellings are double-oriented and they have therefore natural cross ventilation. In the higher levels, they all have a clear view to the west of Paris from the Sacré-Coeur to La Défense. The units are designed

to allow the necessary adjustments at all stages of life, from youth to old age: necessary adjustment in terms of automation to allow home support for seniors in the best possible conditions. Eight apartments are equipped for people with reduced mobility: home automation, automation of all access, lights, and shutters. The comfort of accommodation is also apprehended in all seasons: winter or summer comfort and the relation to the external environment is treated with care both in terms of natural lighting and views.

1. Side view of façade
2. Solar water heat panels on the roof
3. Ground level viewed from garden
4. Garden
5. External wall insulation

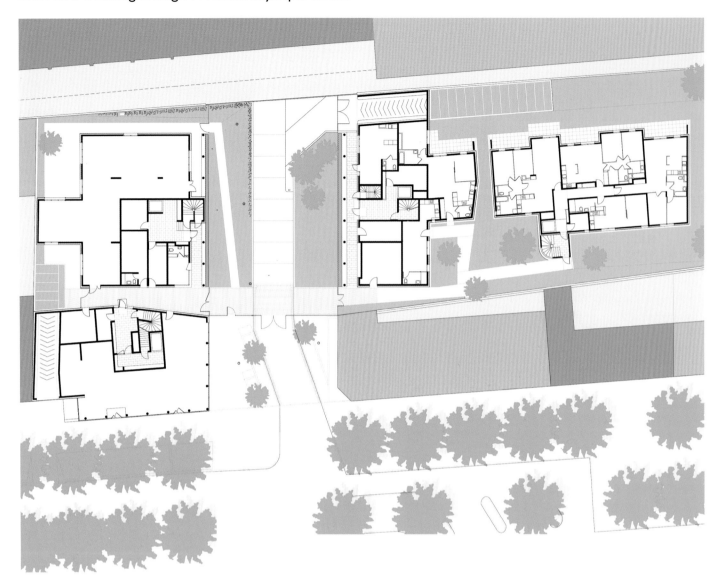

Ground Floor Plan

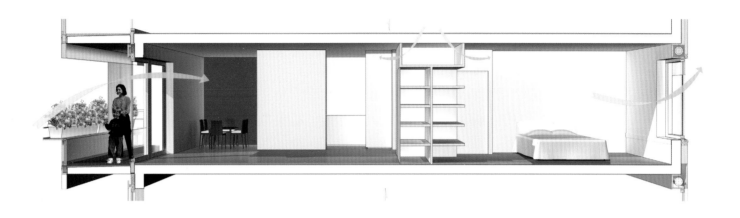

6. Overhang balcony
7, 8. Wall and window details

6

7

8

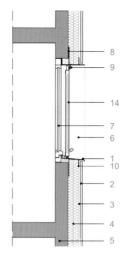

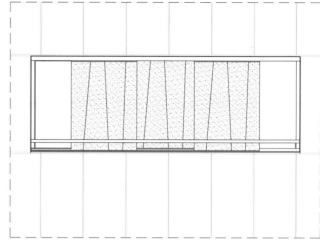

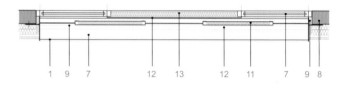

Detail Drawing:
1. 4mm prefabricated aluminium frame
2. Cladding panels: white precast polished concrete (40 mm) or Grey fiber cement (8 mm) or Red laminated board (8 mm)
3. Air space (30 mm)
4. External wall insulation, two crossed layers (15mm)
5. Reinforced concept
6. Balustrade
7. Aluminium window frame
8. Thermal joint
9. Aluminium frames stiffener
10. Extruded polyurethane insulation
11. Folded aluminium sheet
12. Aluminium Prepatined stucco
13. Composite sandwich panel (polyurethane foam)

Sinaloa 193

Location Mexico City, Mexico
Architects Alonso de Garay Urban Lab
Completion Date 2011
Construction Area 2,150m^2
Photos © Jimena Carranza

Sinaloa 193 is a last-century building located in the Colonia Roma. It used to be training centre of Banco del Atlántico, and then stayed in the dropout causing it to be invaded and appropriated by a group of people. Years later it was recovered by the HSBC Bank and released.

The project has 26 apartments on 6 levels, ranging from 56 m^2 to 110 m^2. The architecture aims to be modern but simple, unpretentious, warm and very natural. The architects sought contrasts between industrial and natural elements, with cold textures such as steel and aluminum with warm textures such as stone and wood. The views were not very good so they wanted a landscape design to serve as a curtain, sculptural elements on the idea of recycling scrap pieces heavily polluting materials turned into nests. The courtyards that were once only for the service, are now living gardens with trees and plants, and likewise, much of the roof became green areas.

The landscape design includes traditional species such as the Mexican Nopal. There are also ferns, bamboos, etc. Some plants were chosen according to the theories of Feng Shui such as the Cactus which sought a blue species that represents the strength of winter and without thorns that are regarded as darts or poisoned arrows. Some of the aloe used are rare species endangered in order to develop a habitat for them and promote their preservation.

In short what was sought was the rebirth of a dead century building in the 21st century and used as a space not only for what it was created, housing, but also as a museum of plants, a space for the preservation of species, a home for the waste that pollute our country and an example to follow recycling the city.

Landscape Shades:
1. Tread
2. Aloe
3. Irrigation with storm water
4. Iron wire
5. Old tire
6. Old recycled tires
7. Aloe preservation
8. Pattern
9. Opuntia robusta, cactus variety without thorns

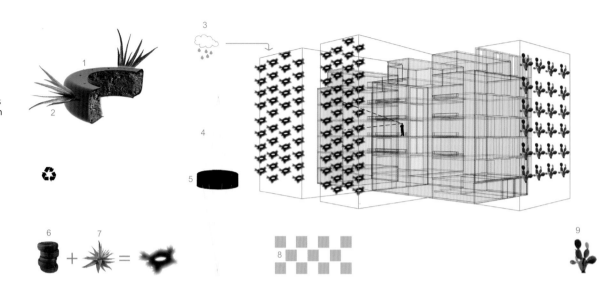

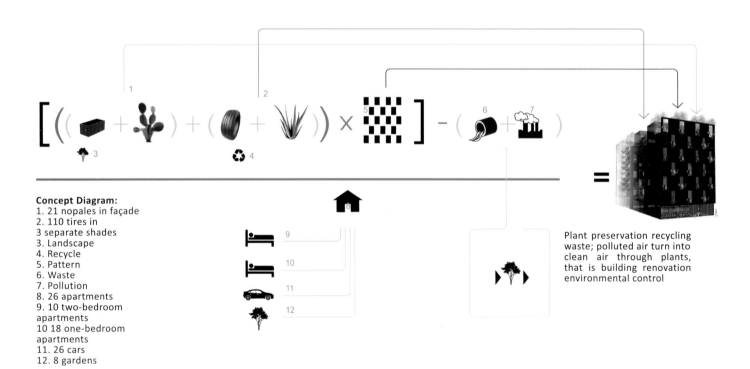

Concept Diagram:
1. 21 nopales in façade
2. 110 tires in
3 separate shades
3. Landscape
4. Recycle
5. Pattern
6. Waste
7. Pollution
8. 26 apartments
9. 10 two-bedroom apartments
10 18 one-bedroom apartments
11. 26 cars
12. 8 gardens

Plant preservation recycling waste; polluted air turn into clean air through plants, that is building renovation environmental control

1. Front façade
2. Entrance detail Atrium detail
3. Entrance detail

Elevation

Section

4-6. Flat interior

Floor Plan:
1. Kitchen
2. Bathroom
3. Living room
4. Dining room
5. Bedroom
6. Terrace
7. Den
8. Storage
9. Family

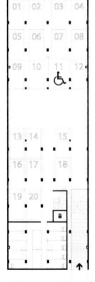
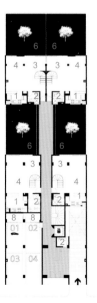
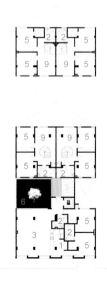
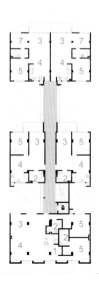

AART architects A/S
www.aart.dk

Alonso de Garay Urban Lab
http://alonsodegaray.mx

Anastasia Arquitetos
www.anastasiaarquitetos.com.br

Andrea Ponsi Architetto
www.andreaponsi.it

Architekturbüro Jakob Bader
www.jakobbader.de

C+S Associati
web.cipiuesse.it

David Elalouf Architecte
www.ade-architectes.fr

GLR arquitectos – Gilberto L. Rodríguez
www.gilbertolrodriguez.com

Jeff Jordan Architects LLC
www.jjarchs.com

Jesse Bornstein Architecture
www.bornarch.com

Johnsen Schmaling Architects
www.johnsenschmaling.com

Seán Harrington Architects
www.sha.ie

Mas Arquitectura
mas.es

Sophie Valla architects
www.sophievalla.nl

nothing architecture (narch)
www.narch.eu

Somosarquitectos
www.somosarquitectos.es

Parque Humano
www.parquehumano.com

Stephen Unger Architects
www.stephen.at

SB Architects
www.sb-architects.com